Why Write in Math Class?

K–5

Linda Dacey

with
Kathleen O'Connell Hopping & Rebeka Eston Salemi

Foreword by Mike Flynn

Stenhouse Publishers
Portland, Maine

Stenhouse Publishers
www.stenhouse.com

Copyright © 2018 by

Library of Congress Cataloging-in-Publication Data
Names: Dacey, Linda Schulman, 1949– author. | Hopping, Kathleen O'Connell,
    1965– author | Salemi, Rebeka Eston, 1958– author.
Title: Why write in math class? : K–5 / Linda S. Dacey, with Rebeka Eston
    Salemi and Kathleen O'Connell Hopping.
Description: Portland, Maine : Stenhouse Publishers, c2018. | Includes
    bibliographical references.
Identifiers: LCCN 2017045003 (print) | LCCN 2017046019 (ebook) | ISBN
    9781625311610 (ebook) | ISBN 9781625311603 (pbk. : alk. paper)
Subjects: LCSH: Mathematics—Study and teaching (Elementary) | Technical
    writing—Study and teaching. | Word problems (Mathematics)
Classification: LCC QA11 (ebook) | LCC QA11 .D2325 (print) | DDC
    372.7/044—dc23
LC record available at https://lccn.loc.gov/2017045003

Cover design, interior design, and typesetting by Martha Drury

Manufactured in the United States of America
PRINTED ON 30% PCW
RECYCLED PAPER

24 23 22 21 20 19 18   9 8 7 6 5 4 3 2 1

Contents

Foreword
by Mike Flynn

hy write in math class? This question has been asked by many teachers, students, parents, and administrators over the years. On the surface, it may seem like writing doesn't have a big role to play in mathematics apart from having students explain how they arrived at a solution to a problem. So much of math class seems to focus on work with numbers, symbols, and shapes, it's hard to imagine finding time for students to write during the math block. Additionally, a number of math curricular materials reinforce this notion by providing few opportunities for students to engage in writing in meaningful ways. However, writing can be a powerful vehicle for student learning in mathematics, and many teachers are finding ways to successfully incorporate it into their classrooms.

The use of writing in math class is receiving a lot of attention lately. There are numerous blog posts and articles discussing why writing in math class is important and how teachers might build more of it into their lessons. Discussions on Twitter feature teachers asking for and/or sharing ideas on how to make writing a focal point during their math blocks. As I dug into this work, I started thinking that it would be really helpful if there was one resource that pulled all of these ideas together in a coherent way so teachers could easily begin implementing them with their students. Imagine how thrilled I was when I found out that Linda Dacey and her supporting coauthors, Kathleen O'Connell Hopping and Rebeka Eston Salemi, were working on a book aimed at doing just that.

I first met Linda a few years ago at an event during the National Council of Teachers of Mathematics Annual Conference and had an opportunity to talk with her about mathematics and learn about her work on this book. I was impressed with her depth of knowledge and her ease at conveying complex ideas so casually in conversation. Not surprisingly, Linda approaches writing with the same ease, and readers will connect with her conversational tone and insightful anecdotes.

In this easily accessible book, Linda makes a strong case for why writing in math class is essential and how it contributes to the learning of students. She then provides a comprehensive look into a variety of options for incorporating writing into the mathematics classroom. Each chapter takes a deep dive into a particular type of writing and includes tangible ideas teachers can implement immediately with their students.

To address the question "Why write in math class?," Linda drew upon her years of experience as an elementary math teacher, a math teacher educator, and a researcher in mathematics education. She also worked with a number of K–5 teachers and math specialists to get a sense of how teachers were successfully using writing in math class. In doing so, she was able to approach the topic from multiple perspectives and provide readers with a broad view of what writing in the classroom looks like across the K–5 range.

Why Write in Math Class? weaves in the work of many innovators and leaders of math education and illustrates how their ideas support the integration of writing in math instruction. For example, in Chapter 4, we see Linda in a fourth-grade classroom incorporating writing using the activity Which One Doesn't Belong? by Christopher Danielson by having students capture their initial ideas before having a class discussion. Later in the chapter, we see how third graders used writing while they engaged in a three-act task created by Graham Fletcher. In Chapter 8, we learn about Kristen Gray's work with math journals as tools for reflection and see how other teachers use them in their classrooms. Linda clearly has her finger on the pulse of what is new and exciting in math class and brings this work into her book to share with readers.

A powerful feature of this book is Linda's use of vignettes throughout the chapters to illustrate how the different types of writing come to life in the classroom. The vignettes include interactions between students and teachers, examples of student work and writing, teacher reflections, and Linda's analysis of what transpired. They provide important examples of what this work looks like in action and serve as models teachers can emulate as they begin this work in their own classrooms.

Whether you are a new teacher seeking resources to help shape your mathematical community of learners or a seasoned veteran looking to spice up your students' experiences in your classroom, you'll find this book incredibly helpful. It is full of concrete ideas, strategies, and resources to support any teacher as he or she looks to integrate more writing in math class. So if you have ever asked the question "Why write in math class?" this book has your answer.

Acknowledgments

I could not have written this book without the generosity and inspiration of many teachers, math specialists, and students.

First and foremost, I want to express gratitude to Kathleen O'Connell Hopping and Rebeka Eston Salemi. Thank you, Kathy and Becky, for coming on this journey with me. As soon as it was confirmed that I would be writing this book, I knew I wanted you to join me. I have appreciated your talent, commitment, and dedication for many years, and throughout this project, my respect for you has continued to grow. I am so glad we were able to work together again and am grateful to your K–5 colleagues and students in the Lincoln Public Schools. Their collaboration was a wonderful gift.

Karen Gartland is another long-standing, admired colleague and friend. Thank you for your written contributions and for reviewing every chapter. Your guidance and insight have always meant a lot to me; I cherish working with you and appreciate the teachers and students in Groton's public elementary schools.

Maureen O'Connell and Jennifer Spencer, thank you for believing in me, inviting me to work with you and the teachers in the Ipswich Public Schools, and being generous with your ideas and support for this book. Sharing professional development experiences with you these past two years has been an incredible learning adventure. I could not have asked for more supportive partners. Thank you to the many teachers at the Paul F. Doyon Memorial School and the Winthrop School who let me observe their teaching, allowed me to teach their students, shared their thinking with me about learning and teaching math, and showed me their students' work. I am enormously grateful to you. I also want to thank principals Sheila McAdams and Sheila Halloran and the William Payne Grant for supporting our work together.

Thank you, Jayne Bamford Lynch, for always being there for me when I need you, and thank you, students at the Baldwin School, a public elementary school in Cambridge, Massachusetts.

Donna Blake, Debbie Carpenito, Marty Daignault, Carolyn Dwyer, Lauren Gouzie, Lina Lopez-Ryan, Lisa Manzi, Lisa Martin, Susan Merrill, Susan Speak, Carol Walker, Melissa Webster, Andrea Welch, and Christine Zybert, I am honored to share your thinking and teaching, and your students' work, with readers so that they can benefit as much as I have.

Thank you to Lucas Daignault and Mark Chubb for permission for their photos to be included and to Graham Fletcher for permission to include his three-act lesson "All Aboard."

I have always been grateful for my relationship with Toby Gordon, Stenhouse managing editor for math and science. Toby, you are a treasured editor, writer, and supporter. Thank you for once again seeing me through the development of a manuscript. I could not be more appreciative of your efforts. You have helped me dig deeper and communicate better.

Kassia Omohundro Wedekind reviewed every chapter, sometimes more than once, and gave me important feedback. Kassia, your insights and suggestions were invaluable. Thank you.

Everyone I have worked with at Stenhouse is amazing: Dan Tobin, Jay Kilburn, Tracy Zager, Stephanie Levy, Laurel Robinson, Louisa Irele, Grace Makley, Chuck Lerch, Zofia McMullin, Chandra Lowe, and Nate Butler. Thank you for your talents!

Finally, thank you, Mike Flynn. I am deeply honored that you agreed to write a foreword to this book.

1 Introduction

Kindergarten teacher Becky Eston Salemi asked a group of children, "Do you know how many letters are in your name?" Clayton appeared perplexed by this question. He looked up and then down as several seconds passed. Meanwhile, the five other children working near him had reached into a basket of linking cubes and were eagerly snapping them together to represent the number of letters in their names. Clayton looked up at Becky and whispered, "I don't know, but if I could write it down, I could count them." She encouraged him to do so, and Clayton proceeded to get a piece of paper and pencil and boldly print the letters in his name. Next, he placed one cube over each letter, touched each cube as he counted from one to seven, and then proudly announced, "I have seven letters in my name!"

Third-grade teacher Jennifer Marino was engaging a small group of students in word study. *Yesterday* was printed on an index card placed in the middle of the table. She modeled how to sound it out by saying each of the three syllables separately and slowly as she pointed to each part of the word. Then she emphasized the three syllables again, but without significant pauses. Finally, she read the whole word quickly. She asked students to turn and talk about what they had observed. Julia turned to her partner and said, "It's just like arrays." Her partner looked confused and asked what she meant. The teacher was also wondering about Julia's thinking, because she had never heard a student connect those two ideas.

Julia began explaining: "They're just the same." When her partner still didn't seem to understand, Julia paused and said, "Wait: it will be easier if I show you in writing." She drew a 3-by-7 array of circles and then drew lines around them to make two smaller arrays: 3-by-3 and 3-by-4. Next, she wrote *yesterday* and drew lines between the syllables. Once she finished her representation (shown in Figure 1.1), she explained, "We chunk it smaller to what we know, and then we find the whole thing. We do it in math and in words."

Figure 1.1
Julia's thinking about arrays and syllables

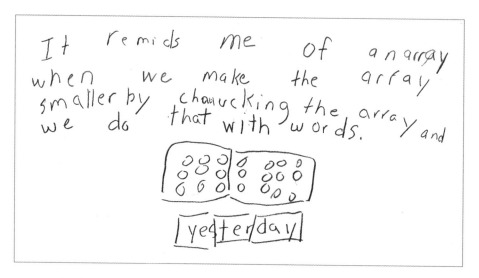

Both Julia and Clayton recognized that writing would be helpful to them. Clayton wrote to help him answer a mathematical question, and Julia wrote to help her communicate relational thinking. Students intuitively recognize the value of writing in math. It makes sense to connect the two. We should build on their natural inclinations to deepen their understanding and their joy of learning mathematics.

Why Do We Want Our Students to Write in Math Class?

An obvious response to this question would be to refer to the learning goals within both mathematics and language arts. In both subject areas, students are expected to communicate their thinking and create arguments that support their ideas (National Governors Association Center for Best Practices, Council of Chief State School Officers 2010a, 2010b). But meeting the standards touches on just some of the goals for weaving writing into math instruction. Writing helps students construct and represent knowledge, make connections between conceptual understanding and procedural fluency, and engage in mathematical communication (Burns 1995; Countryman 1992; Pugalee 2005).

Let's consider how first grader Lila makes representations and connections to communicate her thinking about the following number story:

Dan has 3 strawberries.
Amy gives him some more strawberries.
Now Dan has 10 strawberries.
How many strawberries did Amy give Dan?
Show how you know.

Though it was not required, Lila decided to respond with pictures, numbers, and words (Figure 1.2). She began by drawing two groups of five strawberries. As Lila explained, "I just think about five and five when I see ten." She added dots and leaves to some of the figures to make them look more like strawberries, but then stopped and decided to number seven of them. She did not indicate the separate sets or draw an arrow to show them joining; her picture was her way of exploring the number story, not an illustration of the situation. Lila wrote her equation next, and drew a rectangle around her answer, 7. The number

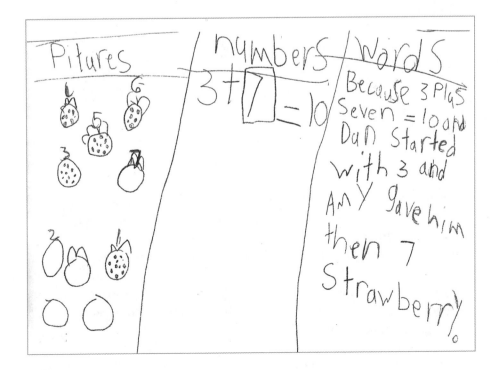

Figure 1.2
Lila's response

sentence mirrors the order of events in the story, and Lila rightfully showed no concern that her answer was the middle number in the equation. Within her "words" section, Lila described the situation using a combination of numbers, words, and symbols.

In *Math in Plain English: Literacy Strategies for the Mathematics Classroom*, Amy Benjamin says, "Writing causes learning. By writing, we create, transform, mobilize, integrate, and secure what might otherwise be fragile knowledge. Writing whips learning into shape!" (2013, xxii). More specifically, writing can help students with the following:

- prepare for a discussion,
- brainstorm what they notice and wonder,
- make connections among multiple representations of ideas,
- explain their thinking,
- clarify their understanding of ideas,
- develop their reasoning skills,
- learn from their mistakes,
- note changes in their thinking over time,
- explore ideas creatively, and
- reflect on their thinking.

Writing also helps teachers with the following:

- gain insights into the variety of students' thinking,
- note partial understandings,
- verify changes in students' thinking over time,
- identify students' mathematical dispositions,
- determine the range of students' understanding,
- develop instructional strategies, and
- engage students in individual written dialogues.

In recent years, we have experienced how talking about mathematics has supported these same objectives. Many teachers have told me how much joy *math talk* has brought to their classrooms, how it has increased students' understanding, helped students learn that mathematical tasks can be approached in many different ways, and provided teachers with important insights into students' thinking. I believe it is time for *writing in math* to join *talking in math* as an important communication strategy for developing, deepening, and assessing mathematical understanding.

What Does Writing in Math Look Like?

Writing can help develop and document ideas. As part of my coming to better understand what writing in math class can look like, I worked with a number of K–5 teachers and math specialists. From the onset of our conversations, one of the first and most resounding questions asked was *What constitutes writing?* These teachers were wrestling with whether simple recordings, graphs, tables, doodles, and so forth meet the criteria for writing in math class. As I listened to their conversations, I came to a firm stance. Yes, they do! As a result, my desire to better understand the role of writing in math class, in all its forms and functions, was kindled. This book is the result of that endeavor.

Determining what we educators consider writing becomes particularly important when we think about our younger students. I love these words from Katie Wood Ray and Matt Glover: "Children's book-making is fueled by the same energy they bring to any activity where they are making things—or making things up—during their dramatic play. And in truth, it is no more surprising that a four-year-old would think of himself as a writer and illustrator than it is that he would think of himself as a fireman or an astronaut." They later continue, "Adults, however, are not always so easily swayed. Many will more easily believe Sean is an illustrator than a writer because they have fewer expectations for what it means for him to be an illustrator. His writing identity is harder to sell because his written artifacts don't yet match adult expectations for what someone who knows how to write should be able to do" (2008, 5). No, they don't quite match, but children in the primary grades are emerging writers, and we want to honor their journey. We must support and applaud their early attempts, so young children can grow as writers as well as mathematicians.

We need to encourage and honor such depictions in the intermediate as well as the primary grades. Making drawings, exploring connections among representations, and jotting questions and notes in formats that make sense to students are necessary components of making meaning and should be celebrated at all levels of learning. As we broaden our view of writing, in all its varied styles and stages, we can recognize the powerful effect it can have on our students' learning as well as the joy it can bring to our classrooms.

Different Types of Writing in the Mathematics Classroom

The authors of *Types of and Purposes for Elementary Mathematics Writing: Task Force Recommendations* identified that "Two overarching goals for elementary mathematical writing were central to the task force's recommendations: for students to *reason* mathematically and to *communicate* ideas" (Casa et al. 2016, 4). With these goals in mind, the task force identified four types of writing, each having a different purpose:

- exploratory writing to make sense of a task;
- informative/explanatory writing to describe or explain;
- argumentative writing to construct or critique a justification, and
- mathematically creative writing to express originality, fluency, and flexibility or to elaborate one's thinking.

A chapter is devoted to each of these types of writing, as well as reflective writing, which the report does not highlight as a separate category. Also, my interpretation of mathematically creative writing differs. The report focuses on particularly creative responses to math tasks. I want to connect math to creative and poetic writing, as well as to encourage creative responses within all formats.

About This Book

Reviewing and analyzing the responses elementary students generate when engaged in mathematical tasks has been a cornerstone of my work with teachers. Within my courses and workshops, written work created by K–5 students provided evidence that teachers and I could consider together as we further developed our understanding of students' thinking. It prompted discussions of learning trajectories, best instructional practices, and assessment data. Here I want to focus on how we can support students' writing about math and how such writing helps develop and deepen their mathematical thinking. Simultaneously, of course, each piece of written work provides an artifact for formative assessment.

In Chapter 2, I look at what we know about teaching writing and forming classroom communities that support communication. I'm hopeful you can apply this knowledge to support writing about math.

Part of successful writing is dependent on developing proficiency with the language of mathematics. Chapter 3 emphasizes students using numbers, symbols, and pictures to communicate their thinking, as well as the development of mathematical vocabulary.

The next five chapters focus on specific purposes of writing about mathematics. Each includes classroom vignettes, learning activities, and samples of student work. Exploratory writing, the kind of writing that helps students delve into initial ideas and begin to make sense of them, is the focus of Chapter 4. Chapter 5 is about explanatory writing. Through a focus on describing or explaining procedures, patterns, visual representations, and mathematical ideas, this type of writing provides ways for students to both communicate and solidify their thinking.

Chapter 6 looks at argumentative writing. It is through this type of writing that students learn how to stake and justify their claims. It is important that we support the writing of mathematical arguments at the K–5 level, because it is the foundation for writing proofs.

Chapter 7 focuses on creative and poetic writing, where students make new connections, pose their own problems, and investigate different literary formats. Chapter 8 considers reflective writing, focusing on how it helps students better understand the choices they make and recognize their growth.

Though these chapters focus on different types of writing, there is often significant overlap among the categories. I found that for a variety of tasks given to students, the direction could be *explore, describe, explain,* and/or *justify.* An argument might include a description and an explanation, or a description might include creative or reflective writing. Aspects of exploratory writing may underpin all written tasks. I find the image of Russian nesting dolls helpful here; you can't get to the smallest doll until all the others have been opened. Each is a separate doll, and yet combined, a new whole is formed. There is something to behold in the collective nature of the dolls, and the packing and unpacking of them remind me of the ways students, and their teachers, work and rework to build mathematical understanding and competence.

2 Developing a Community of Math Writers

Number talks—and math talk, in general—have unleashed a fountain of knowledge about how students think mathematically. These conversations have transformed school mathematics from the memorization of teacher-modeled procedures to the exploration of a variety of approaches that students create and understand. It has transformed math class into a time of active engagement and discovery (Chapin, O'Connor, and Anderson 2003; Kazemi and Hintz 2014; Parrish 2014). Most important, this practice has strengthened students' conceptual understanding and their ability to view themselves as mathematicians. I believe writing provides us with another powerful vehicle for helping students become better mathematical thinkers. It allows us to capture the thinking of every student and the ability to linger over their written responses. When we give students the time to explore their ideas in writing and the freedom to write in their own voices, it can be as engaging and joyful as talking about math.

In Christine Zybert's first-grade classroom, recording the weather on a bar graph is part of the daily class meeting. The student leader fills in a space on the weather graph to indicate whether it's sunny, partly sunny, cloudy, rainy, or snowy outside. The graph for January is shown in Figure 2.1. Note that they record the weather only for the days they are in school; Christine prefers to focus on data they can confirm together.

Figure 2.1
Weather
graph for
January

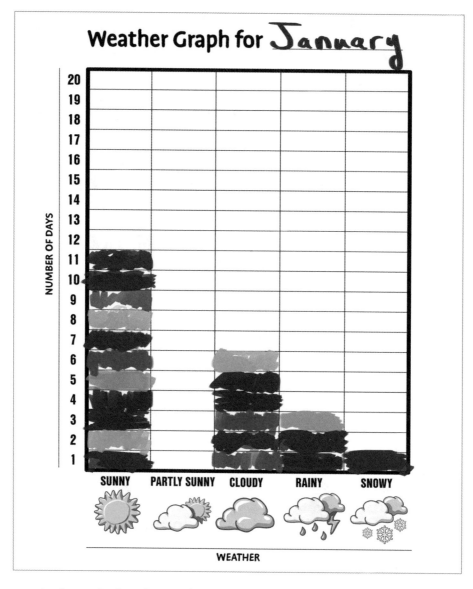

At the end of each month, students consider the completed graph. In September, they respond orally to the simple question *What do you notice about our weather this month?* Over the course of the fall, they begin to respond in writing to such questions as *How many days were sunny? How many more days were cloudy than rainy?* After the last day was marked in a recent January graph, Christine projected four questions for students to consider:

➡ How many days of each type of weather were there?
➡ How many more sunny days were there than snowy days?

➥ Together, how many cloudy and rainy days were there?

➥ How many days did we mark the weather this month?

She gave the students a blank piece of paper along with a copy of the graph.

These questions are standard, often shown on worksheets below a given graph and with blanks in which students are to record their answers. Using their own data, rather than a graph created for them, and blank paper transforms the assignment by making it more meaningful and giving students greater responsibility for how they will respond. This task has also become a familiar routine, which gives them some comfort and confidence.

The students returned to their seats eager to begin. Rosie and Kaydee looked at the graph and had the following conversation:

> *Rosie*: There are lots of sunny days.
> *Kaydee*: Yeah. How are you going to start?
> *Rosie*: I am going to show what happened.
> *Kaydee*: I want to make it like a picture.

Their responses are shown in Figure 2.2. Both of these students have recorded their thinking and provided accurate answers. They have each made connections among visual information, numbers, symbols, and words. Notice how both use drawings and words as labels, perhaps following what was shown on the graph.

figure 2.2
Kaydee's and Rosie's responses

Kaydee

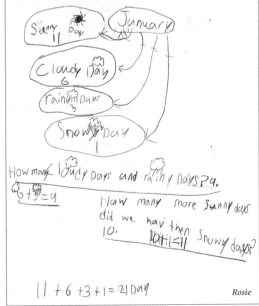

Rosie

Early in the fall, math specialist Carol Walker gave second grader Summer a picture of two collections of base ten materials and asked which pile had more. Her work is shown in Figure 2.3. Notice that Summer decided that it would be helpful to label the two piles, and has personalized the task by using her own initials to do so. Her identification of the number represented by each set of blocks suggests that she needed an exact count to make a comparison. In the section explaining how she knew, however, she offers us another view of her thinking when she refers to the number of tens in each group. If further writing hadn't been required, Carol might not have known that Summer recognized the importance of tens.

Similar to when we listen to students talking about math, we may be surprised by what's revealed when we read their responses. We may uncover unknown partial understandings or advanced mathematical connections. Advanced thinking can be particularly easy to miss if we don't encourage stu-

Figure 2.3
Summer's response

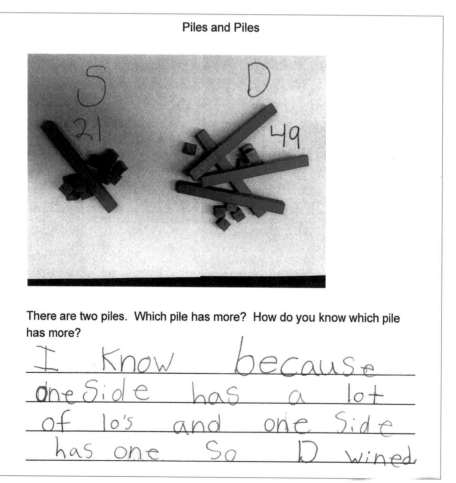

Piles and Piles

There are two piles. Which pile has more? How do you know which pile has more?

I know because one side has a lot of 10's and one side has one So D wined

dents to write about tasks that are challenging enough to stretch their thinking. First-grade teacher Susan Merrill asked me for a story problem for Stephen, a student she thought could consider tasks more difficult than she was providing. I gave her the problem that follows this paragraph. Note that it is the reasoning, not the size of the numbers, that makes this task particularly more challenging. Before reading further, I encourage you to take a moment to solve it. How did you approach it? How did you know your answer was accurate?

> *What's the Number?*
> Jo added the number to 5.
> Chris subtracted it from 13.
> They got the same answer.
> What was the number they used?

I had expected Stephen to use a guess-and-check approach, adding a number to 5 and then checking to see if he got the same answer when he subtracted it from 13. Instead, he quickly answered, "Four." When Sue asked him how he got that answer, Stephen merely shrugged. Sue encouraged him to write about his ideas so that she could learn more about his thinking. Stephen's response (Figure 2.4) suggests he recognized that because 5 plus 8 is 13, the distance between 5 and 13 is also 8. Presumably, because an equal change happened from each endpoint, he identified half of 8—4—as his answer. Sue was quite surprised. She said, "It took me a long time to understand what he did and why it worked, and he got his answer almost immediately. And I never would have known if I hadn't been able to read and visualize his thinking. In fact, I'm not sure he knew exactly what he had done until he was asked to write it down. This writing was important for both of us."

How do we create classrooms where recording thinking and sharing written responses is the norm and facilitates learning for teachers and students? Fortunately, elementary school teachers are quite familiar with ways to teach writing and are learning ways to create communities of math talkers.

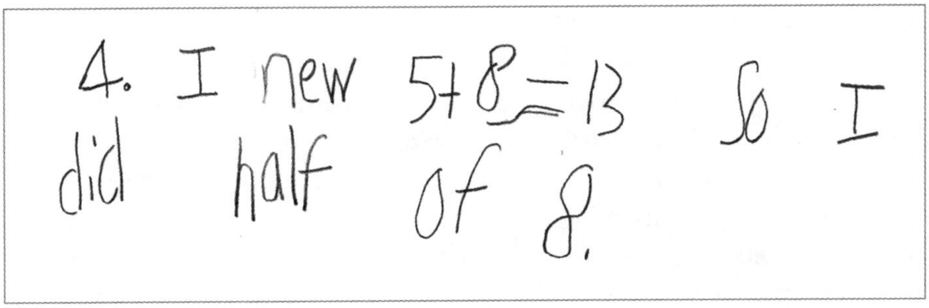

figure 2.4
Stephen's response

Teaching Writing

How we teach writing in today's elementary classrooms is derived from the revolutionary thinking in the late 1960s. For more than half a century, countless researchers and educators have worked tirelessly to offer students a time and a place to find their voices and shape their thinking on paper. It is worth considering how this knowledge might inform our approach to writing about mathematics.

The Writing Process

Donald Graves, Donald Murray, Lucy Calkins, and many other accomplished educational researchers have offered teachers a lens through which to consider the craft of writing. They have delineated a process by which writers go about their work. In the simplest form, there are three stages: prewriting, writing, and rewriting (Murray 1969). Over time, the number of stages has been expanded to five: prewriting, drafting, revising, editing, and publishing. Though it is recognized that there is no one way to write, these stages illuminate the process. By engaging students in each stage, teachers are able to instruct, support, nudge, and celebrate students as writers.

You might wonder how you could possibly find the time to implement what you know about teaching writing during math class. Although I find it important to remember the power of the writing process, not all written work needs to proceed through each of the five stages. For instance, prewriting may often consist of exploring an idea as a class or with a partner. Editing may be limited and perhaps even restricted to corrections made to first drafts as they are written. Finished products in literacy learning may look different from those in math. Publication of math writing may be as simple as sharing responses with peers sitting nearby, presenting them on a document camera for all to see, or simply submitting work to the teacher.

Writing Workshop

Writing instruction may be called a variety of names such as writing workshop, writer's workshop, or simply writing. Regardless of the terminology, certain hallmarks make writing programs a positive force in elementary classrooms. First and foremost is the belief that all children are writers and that it is their teachers' job to help them find their voice and hone their craft. From the kindergartner who painstakingly draws a picture of his new baby sister, labels the drawing with a big red heart to show how much he loves her, and writes 5 to show how many people are now in his family to the fifth graders working on their third draft of a proposal to establish a school garden, there is nothing like the authenticity of watching a child develop as a writer. From mini-lessons to author's chair, every moment is filled with ways to support and honor the growth and development of each writer.

As with the writing process, it is important that we hold this aspirational vision of writing while recognizing that writing about math will not always replicate it, nor does it need to. Though we want to strive for the same level of engagement, individualized instruction, and productivity, it is difficult to imagine students working on the same piece of math writing for a few weeks, or even one week, unless it's related to a major project. Still, we can apply many aspects of writing instruction to math class.

Students are expected to function at a certain level of independence during writing workshop. Selecting their own topic, working at their own pace, deciding when to add illustrations to better convey their messages, taking responsibility for their work space and materials, dating their work, and organizing their efforts are just some of the routines that students need to internalize. Although specific writing assignments may often be chosen for students in math class, the goal is still to have them become the drivers of their written product. It is the students who are eventually in charge of what is written on the paper, how they engage in the writing process, and how they will respond to feedback received from others. We need to believe and help students believe that they can craft their own math narratives.

It is delightful to read authentic voices in students' writing about math. Consider second grader Kat, who has been shown a number line with the numbers one and one thousand marked and asked where she would place one hundred. (Note that a similar task with a number line showing one and one million is discussed in Chapter 8.) As she explains her thinking (Figure 2.5), Kat includes the phrase *that would be silly*. As I read it, I felt as if I could hear the lilt and conviction in her voice. By underlining *would not fit*, she drives her response home.

What Can We Learn from Talk About Math?

How often do you write in a roomful of other writers? How often do you publicly read something you have written, with or without time to practice? For many adults, such tasks would be daunting, and yet, we ask elementary students to do them all the time. How do we create a space in which children feel confident writing and sharing their work with others? Fortunately, we can build on habits students develop when they talk about math.

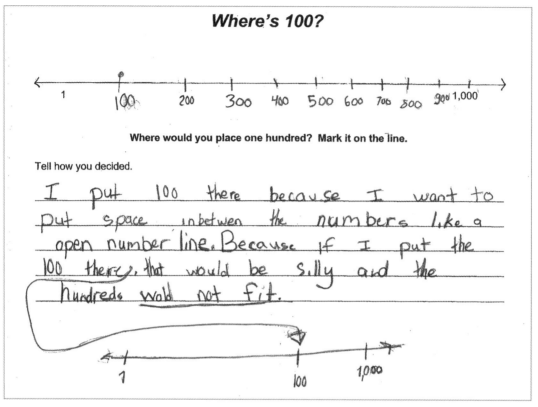

Where's 100?

Where would you place one hundred? Mark it on the line.

Tell how you decided.

I put 100 there because I want to put space inbetween the numbers like a open number line. Because if I put the 100 there, that would be silly and the hundreds wold not fit.

Figure 2.5
Kat's description of how she decided

Supporting and honoring mathematical discourse in classrooms did not happen overnight. Teachers who wanted to meet this goal needed to change several of their behaviors. They needed to stop telling, pose tasks worth talking about, and establish norms for participating in mathematical conversations. Various forms of professional learning helped them. Math specialist Maureen O'Connell told me, "In my school, watching videos of math talks has been invaluable. It gave us a shared vision of what math discussions could look like in classrooms. As we saw what teachers did to stimulate and support conversations, we understood better what we could do. And watching the engagement of students was inspiring."

Students now frequently share their thinking aloud. They have learned to respect one another by giving each other airtime to convey ideas, without interruption, so that everyone can make connections to what someone else has said. They have discovered it is acceptable and sometimes beneficial to change their thinking after learning about the ideas of others. Most important, they have come to realize that diverse thinking is respected and valued. This is a wonderful platform upon which students can build similar comfort when writing about math.

The transfer won't be automatic. Just as with number talks, students will need to learn how to express their ideas in writing, share their written work with others, and respond to what others have written. For some, writing might feel riskier. A comment made in a partner conversation or a gesture used to communicate agreement during a number talk is fleeting and perhaps soon forgotten. Yet it is permanence that adds to writing's power, that allows both teachers and students to review and reflect on previous thinking.

So how do we support students who find writing a somewhat risky activity? Jo Boaler, a Stanford University professor of education, suggests we tell students that research in neurological science has shown that our brains "grow" when we make mistakes (Boaler 2015). When students understand that mistakes are helping them learn, they are far less afraid to make them. Through the youcubed website (https://www.youcubed.org), many teachers have learned of this research and incorporated the notion of growing brains into their classrooms.

Recently, I observed a class of second graders doing a clothesline activity. Students began by estimating the number of steps it would take to walk across their classroom, writing their estimates on a "tent card," and placing the cards, in order, on the clothesline. I know that when I am a participant in a workshop, it feels riskier to write and display my estimate of something than to say it or record it privately. I can feel vulnerable as I display what may be a significant error in thinking. I was reflecting on those feelings when I heard the following conversation:

"I don't know how many steps there are. How can I write it down and put it on the line?" Jason asked.

His partner responded, "Just make a guess."

Jason explained, "But if I am really wrong, everyone will know."

This time his partner laughed and said, "If you make a big mistake, they will know your brain grew bigger."

With that reminder and support, Jason smiled and recorded his estimate. I smiled and reminded myself to learn that lesson as well.

Writing Materials

No doubt you think carefully about the writing materials you offer in literacy learning. Though basic writing tools should be available at all times during math, teachers also consider which supplies they want to highlight or provide in conjunction with specific writing opportunities. Should paper be lined or blank? Should students use single sheets or sheets in a notebook?

Figure 2.6
Kindergarten
students
writing and
illustrating
stories about
the number
of beavers in
a pond

Here are some guidelines about writing materials:

- Kindergartners initially require a lot of space for drawing within their written recordings, so blank paper is often best. As students progress, it can be beneficial to provide paper that offers both open space and lines (Figure 2.6), though we should never overestimate the power of blank paper at all grade levels.

- Two-column paper can stimulate students to write both *what* and *why*.

- Because writing in a notebook can feel more private than writing on a single sheet of paper, reflective writing is often done in a journal. Such a notebook can also keep the work together, supporting the ability to compare thinking over time.

- Crayons or markers should be available to students as well as pencils. Colored pencils can help students distinguish the steps they used to solve a problem or to distinguish peer feedback from original text.

- Rulers and graph paper can support the inclusion of clear diagrams in students' writing.

- Some students often use whiteboards, particularly when they're writing in the rug area. When raised, these boards allow teachers to quickly scan responses. Because the writing is not permanent, some teachers take a picture of a board if they want a written record of a student's thinking.

- If tablets are readily available, students can use them to take a picture of a representation made with manipulatives and then add text to explain their model.

This list of guidelines is not meant to be comprehensive; you may prefer other options or simply wish to have a variety of supplies available to students at all times. Some classrooms use notebooks for everything, capturing all types of writing in math class. What is essential is thinking about which tools best meet the intended writing purpose, are developmentally appropriate, and fit your students' needs. And most important, we must recognize that the limited space provided on many "worksheets" and in workbooks is rarely, if ever, adequate.

Teachers sometimes provide scaffolding through writing prompts and pages. It can be challenging to decide how to support students' writing without taking away their ability to make independent choices. I often hear teachers discuss questions such as these:

- *Should I provide a sentence frame or a template?*
- *Should I provide three lines to help students recognize that there are three possible answers?*
- *Do I need to tell students to explain their thinking, or should I just expect them to do so?*
- *Should I provide labels such as* Pictures, Words, *and* Symbols *at the top of the page?*

Because students' writing needs and purposes differ, I've included a variety of formats in these chapters. Students can also learn to create the support they need; for example, some students will choose a blank piece of paper and then draw lines on the part of the page where they wish to use words.

In the following reflection, kindergarten teacher Becky Eston Salemi captures some of her thinking about what she offers students.

Becky's Reflection

In preparing response/recording sheets for my students, I sometimes spend significant time deciding on the most optimal type of paper for use during math workshop. In talking with my colleagues, I have learned that they, too, struggle with what to offer their students. We may be putting too much weight on this step of the planning process, but every year we revisit this dilemma when offering our young students open-ended problems such as these:

I went apple picking.
I picked 6 apples.
I picked some green apples and some red apples.
How many of each could I have picked?

We have seen such problems posed with space indicated for each possible combination of addends. We know we do not want to use such a format, because we want students to be responsible for deciding whether their responses are complete. At first students tend to just share one or two possibilities, but as we revisit problems of this type, they identify more options. At the end of the year, it is rewarding to see that many students feel certain that they have found all the possible combinations. We would never want to deprive them of this accomplishment.

Formative Feedback

Writers share their work with others to get feedback that will help them improve. In writing workshop, writers share drafts with peers and teachers. The same should be true for writing in math class. Common vehicles for giving formative feedback include conferring with students, what Lucy Calkins refers to as voice-overs, and peer reviews.

As teachers, we know that feedback is important, but it can be challenging to know what type of feedback to give or to find the time to give it. And yet, research indicates that feedback can be one of the most powerful ways to increase learning (Hattie 2008). Grant Wiggins defines *feedback* as "information about how we are doing in our efforts to reach a goal" (2012, 10). He also contrasts feedback with comments that are judgmental or advisory. Goal-related feedback is descriptive and relates directly to a clear objective. Comments that offer judgments or advice are avoided because they can cause learners to develop a lack of trust in their own judgment or to simply shut down. Similarly, Universal Learning by Design guidelines recommend mastery-oriented feedback—that is, feedback that guides learners to mastery and encourages perseverance (CAST 2011).

Consider the following three examples of feedback that could be given to a student about including a tape diagram (bar model) in his or her response.

Goal related: I noticed that you accurately used a tape diagram as your way of representing the problem.

Judgmental: I like seeing that you used a tape diagram to represent the two numbers you are comparing in this problem.

Advice: You should make a tape diagram to represent this problem.

Note that the goal-related comment clearly says what has been accomplished. It is specific, rather than a general statement such as *Good job!* The judgmental statement suggests the importance of pleasing the teacher, and the advice suggests there is only one way to represent a mathematical idea. Because the point of feedback is to help a student learn, we want to emphasize goal-related information along with encouragement. You may want to reflect on the feedback you give your students over the next few days and consider whether it does the following:

➡️ relates to a specific learning goal,
➡️ encourages perseverance and the belief that the student will reach mastery, and
➡️ gives specific examples of how a student has improved toward meeting a goal.

Conferring

Conferring with students about their writing is an art unto itself. Sitting beside a student, listening wholeheartedly to his or her piece, while withholding judgment, is no easy task. It can be challenging not to jump in and tell students how to make their work more precise or persuasive, but the role of the teacher in this situation (and most others) is first and foremost to listen and then to ask questions or make specific observations.

Figure 2.7
Third-grade teacher Debbie Carpenito conferring with students on their writing about arrays

A teacher might begin by asking students to describe what they are working on. They may take a minute to read the piece, or part of a piece, a student is drafting so they can provide formative feedback quickly. Sometimes teachers have a goal in mind that they want to share with the child. They might offer an observation and a question by saying, for instance, "I notice you have been working on using more descriptive language. Can you show me part of your piece that you feel good about?" Sometimes these conversations are very specific and offer direct and explicit instruction, and sometimes they start with a general and sincere "Tell me what you are working on."

This same approach can be applied when students are writing in math class. You may first want to focus on the student's conceptual understanding of the mathematical idea and then consider the clarity of his or her response. Questioning strategies are most important if your goal is to help the writers uncover their partial understandings and inaccuracies as well as improve their abilities to communicate their thinking. Sample questions are suggested in Table 2.1.

Informal Voice-Overs

Lucy Calkins and Amanda Hartman use the term *voice-over* to describe a type of interaction many teachers use in their classrooms to manage student engagement and provide feedback while "not asking every child to stop, freeze, and look at you. Instead, you (the teacher) are talking like a sportscaster above the hubbub" (2013, 14). For example, when a teacher notices that almost all students are working alone and wants to encourage working with others, she might choose to say something such as "As you begin to solve this problem, remember you can work alone, with a partner, or in a small group." When students hear this feedback, they do not have to completely stop what they are doing, but may make adjustments to better meet their needs.

Other voice-overs may support students by nudging their thinking. Here are some examples:

- *I just noticed that one group is using chart paper and different colored markers to show their steps.*
- *Be sure to show what steps you take to arrive at your solution as well as your answer.*
- *Some students are using a table to represent their work. Is a chart, graph, or table something you want to consider?*
- *If you have arrived at a solution, stop for a moment and consider whether it makes sense to you.*
- *I see some students are making an estimate to help them get started.*

Table 2.1 Possible questions to ask in a conference	
Open-ended questions to begin a conference	How's it going? What would help you right now? What can you tell me about your explanation? What part of your description do you feel the best about? What challenges have you faced so far?
Questions to prod further thinking	What else do you know about this? Have you told why as well as what? What do you still wonder about? What do you think you should work on next?
Questions to generate further clarity	Could someone else understand your thinking? How might a drawing support your thinking? Are there other steps you could include? Is there an example that you think would be helpful? Are there other details you think the reader needs? How might labels help?
Questions to draw attention to precision	Have you tested your idea? Have you checked your computation? How have you used the equals sign? Is there math vocabulary you should include?
Questions to end a conference	How would you summarize your next step? How has your thinking changed since you started this task? What did you learn by writing this? What might you do differently next time? How are you thinking about yourself as a mathematician?

Though each of these remarks could be made to an individual or small group during a formal or informal conference, a voice-over allows everyone to consider and make use of them, if they make sense at that moment. Be strategic with your use of voice-overs and mindful not to say too much. Be careful of the timing of your comments; you do not want to sidetrack your students or derail their productivity. Voice-overs should not present new content, and they work best when they connect to the current lesson. Like any form of feedback, they are intended to increase performance and deepen understanding.

Peer Reviews

Peer feedback can be an effective way to improve student writing and engage students in the writing process. Potentially, both the writer and the reviewer learn from the process. There are a variety of ways in which students can give feedback:

- Conduct a gallery walk in which students "tour" written work the way they would an art gallery and then gather as a group to share general comments about what they noticed. For example, a student might say, "I noticed that a lot of people included a drawing, and I think that is a good idea." Or, prompt specific noticing with a direction such as "As you take your gallery walk, leave a note about how ideas are represented."
- Students can write compliments and suggestions on a sticky note and attach it to a piece of work. If they're presented with the work on a computer, they can give feedback using the comment feature of the text editor.
- Have students complete a comment sheet that provides specific questions for editors to answer, such as *What did you learn?* or *What confused you?* Sentence stems such as *I wondered . . . I noticed . . .* and *My favorite sentence was . . .* can also be used.
- Students can share their writing with a partner and then have a conversation.
- Ask students to focus on a specific aspect of the task, such as math vocabulary.

Regardless of the format they use, students need to learn how to review the writing of their peers, just as they had to learn how to comment on the thinking of others in number talks. I love hearing students incorporate phrases such as *I agree with _____, but I also noticed . . .* in their math discussions. Teaching how to critique the writing of others is often included in literacy learning. We can build on this knowledge, though transfer of this skill to math writing cannot be assumed.

Fourth-grade teacher Carolyn Dwyer introduced this idea to the whole class by reviewing a piece of writing about how a problem was solved. She began by asking, "What do you think the writer did well?" After students had generated a few ideas, she said, "Giving a positive statement can be a good way to begin our reviews." Next, Carolyn wanted the students to give suggestions to the writer. They began by discussing the importance of the tone of the suggestions we make to others. She said, "The way we make suggestions can make a big difference." She showed them a list of comments (Figure 2.8) and asked, "What might be a better way to make these comments so that the ideas are more likely to be heard?"

Figure 2.8
Comments to be restated to be more effective

You've made this so confusing!
You need to redo this.
This is horrible work.
You are so careless.
Is this all you have to write?
This math is wrong.

There was some laughter as the sentences were read, and then students practiced making "I statements," offering specific suggestions, asking questions, and demonstrating a respectful tone. For example, *You've made this so confusing* became *I had some trouble understanding what you meant here. Is there a picture you could make?* Then they returned to the writing sample and shared comments. After this mini-lesson, Carolyn asked students to work in pairs to review the problem explanations they had written the day before. Three examples of peer responses are shown in Figure 2.9. Note that the third one also indicates that the student learned from the opportunity to conduct a peer review.

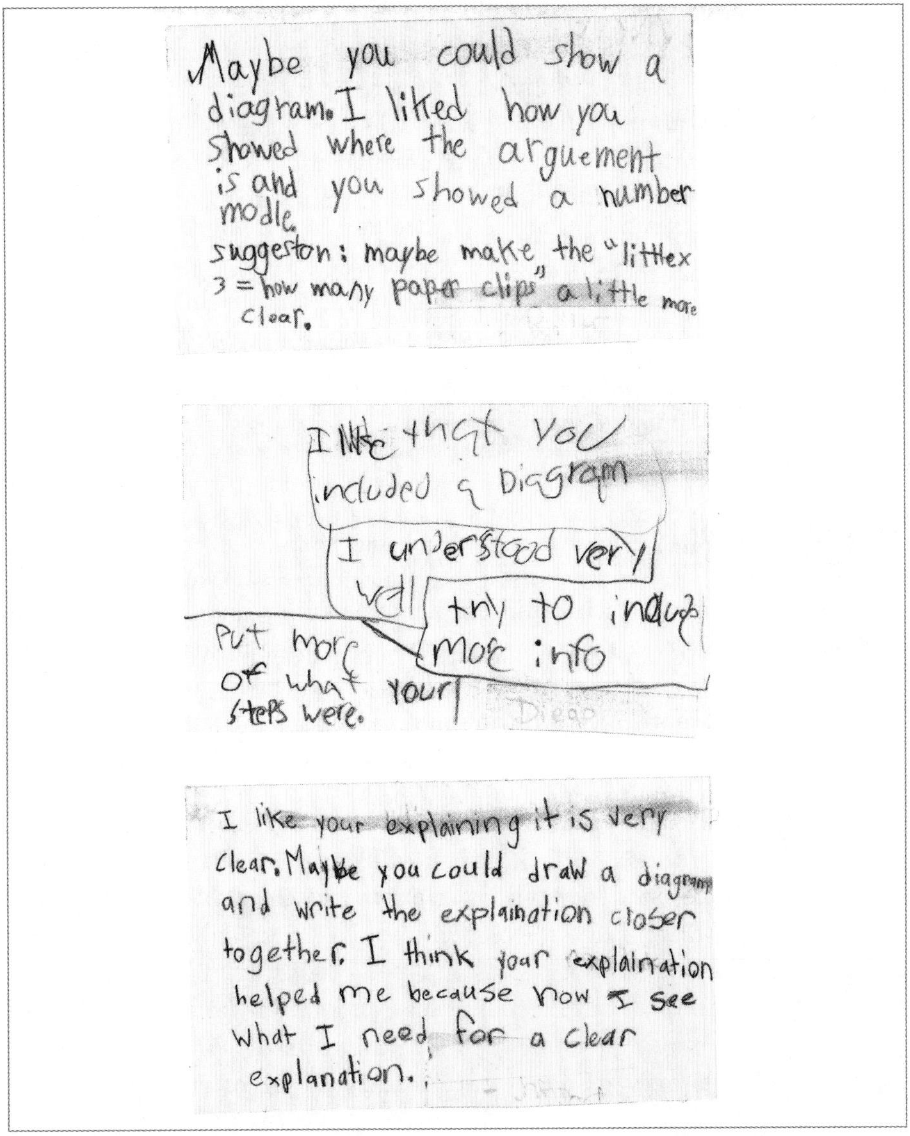
Maybe you could show a diagram. I liked how you showed where the arguement is and you showed a number modle.
suggeston: maybe make the "littlex 3 = how many paper clips" a little more clear.

I like that you included a Diagram
I understood very well
try to include more info
Put more of what your steps were.

I like your explaining it is very clear. Maybe you could draw a diagram and write the explaination closer together. I think your explaination helped me because now I see what I need for a clear explanation.

Figure 2.9
Peer review comments

Holding High Expectations for All

One of the keys to the success of writing workshop is belief in the ability of all students to become writers. Sadly, we continue to see that this steadfast belief in our students does not always carry over into math class. For years, many parents, teachers, and learners have believed that some people just can't do math and that those who can are incredibly smart. Such beliefs have kept many learners from experiencing the joy of mathematics. Carol Dweck, a professor of psychology at Stanford University, has conducted research on mindset that has helped us understand the effect of different core beliefs on our ability to learn (Dweck 2006). A fixed mindset, with the belief that intelligence does not change, gives learners little motivation to work hard so they can improve. A growth mindset, with the belief that hard work can make us "smarter," allows everyone to believe that they can succeed and that effort is worthwhile.

In addition to a growth mindset about learning mathematics, we must believe and teach our students to believe that we can all learn to write about math ideas and that there is good reason to do so. We need to reframe our stance from *How can we expect all of our students to write about math?* to *How does what I know about teaching writing and facilitating math talk help me foster mathematical writing in all of my students?* This shift in thinking reminds us that a growth mindset applies to teaching as well as to learning.

Closing Thoughts

The ways in which you teach writing in literacy learning can be models for you in math. You can create a classroom culture for writing in math that sets the same high expectations for engagement, allows for risk taking, and provides the same kinds of support offered during number talks. When students develop their own voice as writers about mathematics, they find purpose in writing about the ideas they are striving to understand.

3 Learning *the* Language *of* Mathematics
Numbers, Symbols, and Words

To help students clearly communicate their thinking, we need to provide them with opportunities to learn the language associated with mathematics. Although mathematical language is more than numbers, symbols, and specific words and phrases, those are fundamental to mathematical communication, and so we begin there.

Early Learning of Numbers

Many children come to kindergarten knowing how to rote-count to ten—that is, to say the number names in order. By this age, they also may know that as with the letters of an alphabet, these numbers can be written and *mean* something. Over time, students connect corresponding symbols, number names, and sets of objects. Forming these connections is the initial mathematical focus in most kindergarten classrooms and is one of the first steps students take as they learn to navigate the language of mathematics and our number system. Consider the following classroom vignette that occurred within the first few weeks of school as kindergarten teacher Becky Eston Salemi worked with a group of eight students.

Becky places a bin of cubes in front of the children and asks them to each make a group of five. She gives them time to check that their groups contain exactly five cubes, and then they rote-count to five together. They identify the numbers that come before and after five as they recite the counting sequence once again. The children return their cubes to the bin and Becky shows them a premade poster. She writes the 5, along with the 4 and the 6, emphasizing the phrases The number is, The number before it is, *and* The number after it is *as she does so. Recognizing that this type of language might be unfamiliar to her new students, she asks them to repeat each phrase before they move on. Figure 3.1 shows the poster before and after the mini-lesson.*

Figure 3.1
Posters before and after the mini-lesson

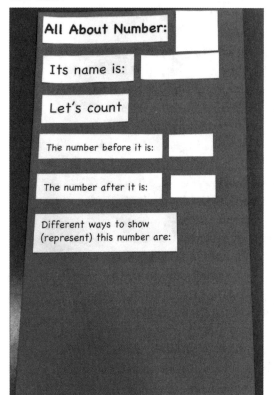

Then Becky gives each student a sticky note and markers and asks them to make a drawing of five objects. After they complete their drawings, each child shares his or her representation before placing it on the poster. As Camille does so, she realizes that she has drawn one too many. She sighs and says, "I guess I forgot to double-check." After a few seconds and a brief exchange with the other students in the group, Camille decides to put an X over one of her apples.

"There, that's better," she says. Matt presents his drawing last. As he does so, he realizes that he has drawn only four objects. "Can I add one more?" he asks. After a nod from Becky, he does so and smiles happily as he displays his edited representation.

Just as in nearly all activities, students displayed a range of development and experience. You can see this in their abilities to draw objects as well as in the organization of their representations. The majority of these students seemed to have a solid sense of five and drew an arrangement that looked similar to how five is shown on a die. Others drew their objects in a more random manner, and one drew them in a line. Most important, the students self-corrected their work. It is wonderful to witness students learning that they can edit work to reflect their new learning. Viewed from this perspective, writing provides students with the means to record their thinking for closer examination and allows for further fine-tuning or elaboration, as appropriate.

Becky's Reflection

When I think of the layers of modeling and thinking that are going on in this activity, I know this is important work for my students. Developing a sense of quantity and the relationships among numbers is at the heart of the kindergarten curriculum. This activity is designed so that students begin to see how recording numbers with a variety of representations is one way to communicate what they know in math. It also supports multiple levels of language development with words such as <u>all, count, number, before, after, show,</u> and <u>represent.</u> I know these are words the children will use over and over again as they explore mathematical ideas across the grades.

When my students work together to fill in the All About Number poster, they share their own thinking in writing and see how it is the same as or different from the responses of their peers. This activity offers them a chance to talk and write about numbers, use familiar and novel mathematical language, see how the same quantity can be represented in different ways, and recognize that a different physical arrangement does not necessarily indicate a different amount. Once everyone in the class has had an opportunity to explore this activity in a small group and learn about the structure and expectation of the task, they can complete individual sheets for any number I assign.

This task is one of a handful of ways that I see writing in math class being introduced and cultivated in kindergarten. I think of it as offering sentence frames about numbers. Young children start writing stories by drawing a series of pictures and then telling and retelling them aloud. In my mind, writing in math class serves the same purpose. Drawing, recording, and representing are the ways my students begin to get their mathematical ideas on paper, share them with others, and explore the language and concepts of mathematics.

Symbols

We frequently use symbols to communicate our mathematical thinking. I continue to be fascinated by the history of numeration and awed by the elegance of our base ten number system. A variety of ways to record numbers have developed over thousands of years, although the equals sign was first introduced less than five hundred years ago. Symbols are abstract, and just as it took many, many years for them to evolve, it takes time for students to fully understand their meaning and record them correctly. Learning the purpose and conventions of these symbolic notations begins at the primary level and continues to develop as students progress through the grades.

Symbols for Numbers

As with letters, it takes time for children to learn how to write numbers correctly. Reversals are commonplace. The symbol for three, for example, may be reversed, perhaps because children are also learning how to write the capital letter *E*, or because their brains do not yet see the orientation as different or significant. Such reversals are not based on conceptual misunderstandings and tend to diminish with instruction, practice, and time. As teachers, we need to think about how often we ask students to correct their reversals. So long as you can follow the intent of the students' writing, should you honor their work and be strategic about when and how often you ask them to make such corrections? Doing so is particularly appropriate when a single digit is reversed, rather than the order of the digits in a multidigit number.

It can be challenging to know if, when a student writes *81* for *18*, it is because of a careless recording, a calculation error, an underdeveloped idea, or a deeper misunderstanding of place value. Patterns within our base ten number system can support students' abilities to read and write numerals with more than one digit, though some types of numbers generally require more attention.

Ten through nineteen, sometimes referred to as the *tricky teens*, are particularly problematic, because these number names do not follow the standard patterns. Consider the following list of inconsistencies:

- For all other two-digit numerals without a zero in the ones place, you first write the digit for the decade name and then write the digit for the ones place, which corresponds to how you hear the number name. But *teen* is said second, not first.
- The number names eleven and twelve do not include a separate name for the ones and tens digits.
- All the other two-digit number names use *ty* to indicate tens, rather than *teen*.
- The number names for thirteen and fifteen do not use the expected names for three and five.

Clearly, we should not be surprised that many students find the teen numbers challenging. The Counting Jar (TERC 1998) is a common number routine in Becky's classroom. She puts sets of small objects in a jar and during math workshop, students are expected to determine the quantity and represent that total. Students then build or draw equivalent sets and may also record numerals to indicate how many they counted.

Johnna and Ben are completing the task together. They count objects, in this case small disks, and agree that there are seventeen. They work independently as they record the quantity. When they finish, Ben looks at Johnna's recording and says, "Wait: my number looks different" (Figure 3.2).

Johnna brings her paper closer to Ben's, looks at both recordings, and says, "That's seventy-one."

Figure 3.2
Ben and his original recording

"Huh?" Ben says, and gets up to look at a nearby chart associated with the number of days in school. He uses the pointer to help him keep track as he counts to seventeen and then says, "Oh, I get it." He returns to where he was working with Johnna and corrects his paper.

Becky observed this interaction and knew that reversing the numerals for the teen numbers was common. She was pleased that Ben had noted the discrepancy between his and Johnna's recordings and knew where to find visual support within the classroom to confirm or correct his work. She also noted the power of writing in this instance: "I have seen students arrive at different counts of their collections and not show any concern. In my experience, that is less likely to happen when students write the numbers. Somehow many of these young students seem to have a greater expectation that when two different students write numerals to tell how many, they need to be the same."

Another challenge for students is learning the name of the next decade. You'll hear students pause or drag out how they say a number such as forty-nine as they search their memory for the name of the decade that comes next. Initially, some students may not completely understand that nine is the greatest digit in any one place and they'll just follow the pattern in the ones place, saying or writing, for example, forty-seven, forty-eight, forty-nine, forty-ten. Here again, our number names *twenty, thirty,* and *fifty* do not help. It is only when we get to sixty that each decade sounds more like its one-digit counterpart.

A color-coded chart summarizing "special" number names is shown in Figure 3.3 so you can consider all the inconsistencies that students need to nav-

Figure 3.3
Color-coded hundreds chart indicating inconsistencies in our number names

1	2	3	4	5	6	7	8	9	10
★11	★12	13	14	15	16	17	18	19	20
21	22	23	24	25	26	27	28	29	30
31	32	33	34	35	36	37	38	39	40
41	42	43	44	45	46	47	48	49	50
51	52	53	54	55	56	57	58	59	60
61	62	63	64	65	66	67	68	69	70
71	72	73	74	75	76	77	78	79	80
81	82	83	84	85	86	87	88	89	90
91	92	93	94	95	96	97	98	99	100

★ no decade name or recognizable ones digit included

decade name is *not* said first

☐ ones digit said differently

● tens indicated by *teen* not *ty*

decade name does not match name for corresponding ones digit

igate between number names and how they are recorded. In written form, however, all two-digit numerals appear to follow the same pattern. I suggest, therefore, that it is through the investigation and the recording of written numerals that the patterns within our number system are best illuminated.

Fortunately, once we get to the hundreds and beyond, things settle down a bit! For example, unlike our names *thirty* for three tens, or *fifty* for five tens, we say *three* hundred or *five* hundred, making it much easier to identify the next hundred when you get to, for example, four hundred ninety-nine. This pattern then continues into infinity. Though consistent, writing these numbers can be challenging when zeros are involved. Some students overgeneralize, concluding that they write a digit for each number they hear. When students hear the word name three hundred four, for example, this misconception may cause them to write either *34* or *3004*. Even students in grades four and five can make such an error when they first begin to work with numbers that have five or more digits. Flipbooks (Figure 3.4) are helpful here, because zeros remain when not covered by another digit or no longer show when a nonzero digit is part of the number.

| Hundred-Thousands | Ten-Thousands | Thousands | Hundreds | Tens | Ones |

Figure 3.4
Picture of a flipbook

When students circle numerals within a multiple-choice format, match numerals to word names, or compare or order numbers written for them, they are merely demonstrating their ability to *recognize* the correct way numerals are printed, not their ability to *write* them. We need to be sure that students across the elementary grades have opportunities to write numerals and connect them to the structure of our number system. Potential tasks include having students do the following:

➡ count large collections of objects and record the totals;
➡ record estimates of large quantities or long distances;

- ➡ listen to a story with several number names, enter them in their calculators followed by the addition sign, and check totals;
- ➡ explore books such as *How Many Jelly Beans?* by Andreas Menotti (2012) or *Greater Estimations* by Bruce Goldstone (2016) that connect visual models to numbers and word names while providing wonderful opportunities to estimate quantities;
- ➡ have a scavenger hunt for particular number words in the news or within informational texts and write the corresponding numerals;
- ➡ complete or create number sentence frames about themselves such as these: *I have _____ cousins. I sleep about _____ hours per night [or week or year]. I can name _____ people I know whose first name begins with a letter before F. If my family were laid end to end, we would measure _____ inches [or centimeters].*

The Equals Sign

Perhaps no symbol in elementary school mathematics is as important or as misunderstood as the equals sign (which can be correctly identified as *equals sign* or *equal sign*). For many years, students were almost always shown equations in which only one number, the answer, was written on the right side of the sign. As a result, many interpreted the equals sign as meaning *write the answer*. This limited understanding of the equals sign can result in students concluding that 13 or 17 is the missing number, when given 5 + 8 = ❑ + 4. Such a fragile understanding of the equals sign can limit the relational thinking that is so important to algebraic reasoning. It's important for students to understand that the expressions on either side of the equals sign have the same value (Kilpatrick, Swafford, and Findell 2001). The idea of "balance" is often suggested. Such thinking would allow a student to determine that because the left side is equal to thirteen, the right side must be as well and think, "What plus four is equal to thirteen?" A student might also reason that since four is one less than five, the missing number must be one more than eight (nine) to have the same value or to keep the balance.

Although this is still an issue, teachers have a growing awareness of this concern, and several curricular materials now show equations in more varied formats—for example, 5 + 13 = ❑ + 12, ❑ = 71 + 63, and 500 = 5 × ❑ × 5. A group of teachers I was working with became interested in whether this exposure had changed students' understanding of the equals sign. In particular, we wondered whether earlier research that suggested that the misconception did not tend to change as students got older (Carpenter, Franke, and Levi 2003) still held true. We decided to pose the question *What does = mean to you?*

Three samples of work from Debbie Carpenito's third-grade classroom (Figure 3.5) are indicative of the majority of the responses we collected. They suggest that students' understanding of the equals sign remains incomplete. Both Charlie and Enrico say that it means to write the answer, with Charlie suggesting that it is relevant only to addition examples and Enrico recognizing its use with all operations. Cleo's response is less definitive, leaving room for a slightly broader interpretation. All of their examples show only one number to the right side of the equation, though Cleo included an alternative in her written section. Debbie was surprised by these responses. Her students had been exposed to a variety of equation formats and had talked about the symbol meaning *the same as* or *have the same value as*. This work doesn't mean the students don't have a broader understanding of

Figure 3.5
Student responses suggesting limited understanding

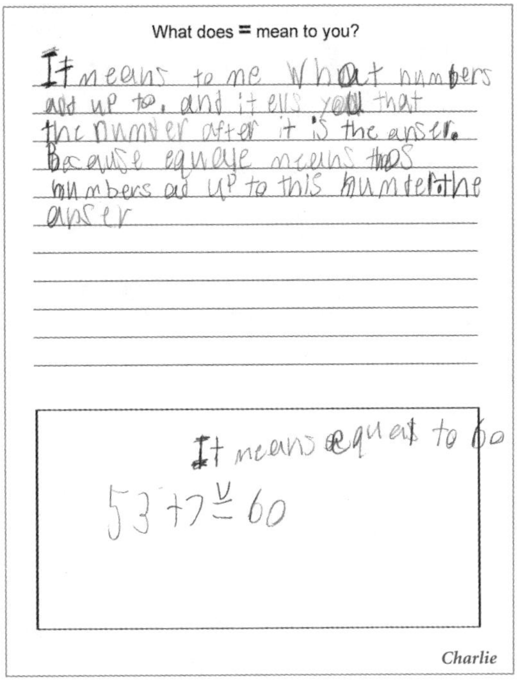

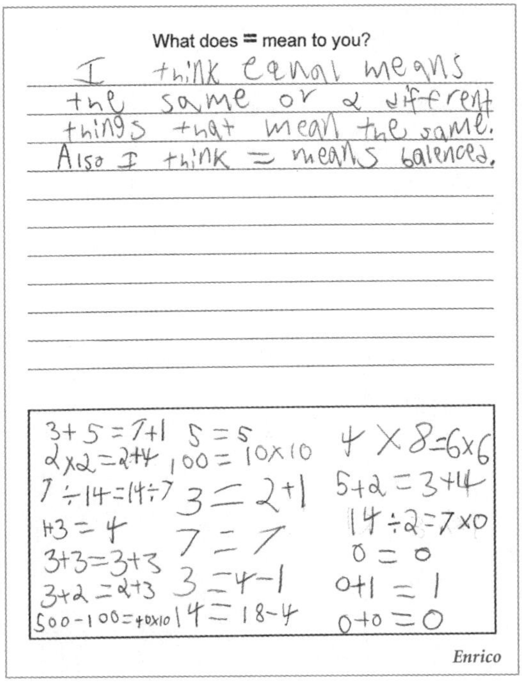

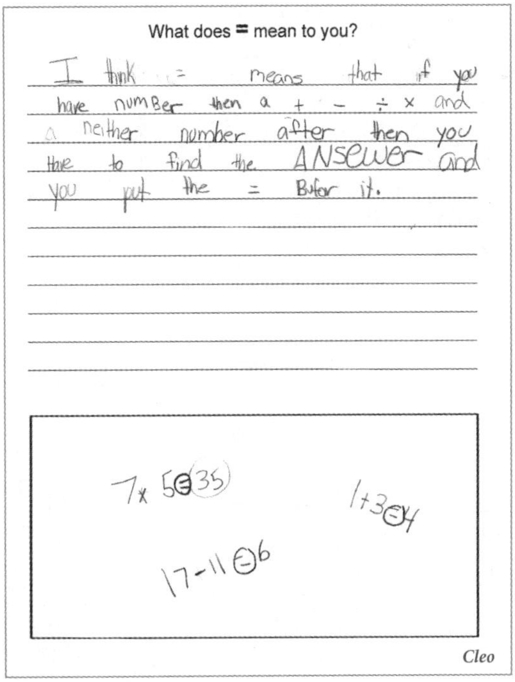

What does = mean to you?

It means to me What numbers add up to, and it tells you that the number after it is the anser. Because equals means that numbers add up to this number the anser

It means equal to 60

$53 + 7 \overset{v}{=} 60$

Charlie

What does = mean to you?

I think eqnal means the same or different things that mean the same. Also I think = means balanced.

$3 + 5 = 7 + 1$ $5 = 5$ $4 \times 8 = 6 \times 6$
$2 \times 2 = 2 + 4$ $100 = 10 \times 10$
$7 \div 14 = 14 \div 7$ $3 = 2 + 1$ $5 + 2 = 3 + 4$
$+3 = 4$ $7 = 7$ $14 \div 2 = 7 \times 0$
$3 + 3 = 3 + 3$ $0 = 0$
$3 + 2 = 2 + 3$ $3 = 4 - 1$ $0 + 1 = 1$
$500 - 100 = 40 \times 10$ $4 = 18 - 4$ $0 + 0 = 0$

Enrico

What does = mean to you?

I think = means that if you have number then a + - ÷ × and a neither number after then you have to find the ANSWER and you put the = Bifor it.

$7 \times 5 \ominus 35$ $1 + 3 \ominus 4$

$17 - 11 \ominus 6$

Cleo

Figure 3.6
Fifth graders' responses

What does = mean to you?

This is what the = sign means to me. It means What the 2,3,4 or more numbers = like 8+6=14 of 14= 4+6. Or you put it there before the answer. It gets put in a eaquation.

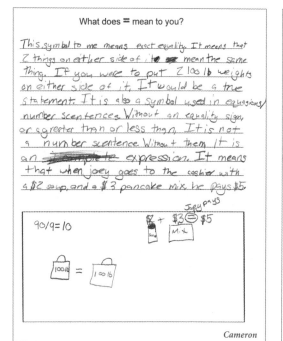

numbers
number
9+20 = 29 ← answer
equal sign

number number
20+8 = 28 ← an wser
equal sign

Leanne

What does = mean to you?

This symbol to me means exact equality. It means that 2 things on either side of it mean the same thing. If you were to put 2 100 lb weights on either side of it, It would be a true statement. It is also a symbol used in equations/ number scentences. Without an equality sign, or greater than or less than, It is not a number scentence. Without them It is an expression. It means that when joey goes to the cashier with a $2 soup and a $3 pancake mix he pays $5.

Joey pays

90/9=10

+ $3 = $5
M.x

100lb = 100lb

Cameron

What does = mean to you?

= means to me equal and /or equivelent. It means the numbers, letters, words, ect. on both sides are equal to each other. or in the case of fractions and decimals it could mean they are equivelent. It could also mean two people are equal, two things are equal, or even two traits are equal.

A is equal to 1
A = 1

½ is equivelent to 0.5
½ = 0.5

House is equal to home
House = Home

A is equal to pencil
= Pencil

Bram

the symbol, only that they didn't demonstrate it here, but it does cause some concern. The point is, checking students' thinking through writing can alert us to possible partial understandings and show us the need for further investigation. It also reminds us that when reviewing their written work, we need to take note of their accurate use of numbers and symbols.

From our informal sampling of two classes at each grade level, it appears that students' understanding of the equals sign does change over time. Three representative responses from fifth-grade students are provided in Figure 3.6. Words such as *balance* and *the same as* replace the idea of it meaning *answer*. Note that Cameron differentiates between equations and expressions. Students are perhaps familiar with the more casual use of the equals sign outside of math class, such as on a poster that reads *Hard Work = Success*, and have included examples with words here.

At this age, students are also studying the notion of equality in their social studies classes. A few students referred to the equality of all people, and one student made us smile when we read *The word* equal *means happiness and having freedom in the world. Equal to me means having balance in my life.* She then added, *But the equals <u>sign</u> means "same as" or "balanced."*

Of course with such a small sample, I can't conclude for certain that there's definite growth with the older students, but along with being surprised by the third graders' limited understanding, I was heartened by the change in fifth graders. You and your colleagues across grade levels may want to pose this question and together consider what students write. Written work provides teachers with access to a greater variety of student responses. It can help us understand students' learning trajectory, place their work within that journey, and note persistent partial understandings.

We also need to be aware that students can misuse the equals sign by creating what I think of as a run-on number sentence. Take a moment to consider how each student uses the equals sign in the two examples shown in Figure 3.7. The example on the top shows a correct use of more than one equals sign, as $5 + 1 = 6$ and $6 = 8 - 2$. The example below it is incorrect because it suggests that each of the expressions have the same value, although they do not. Other examples of this error appear in later chapters.

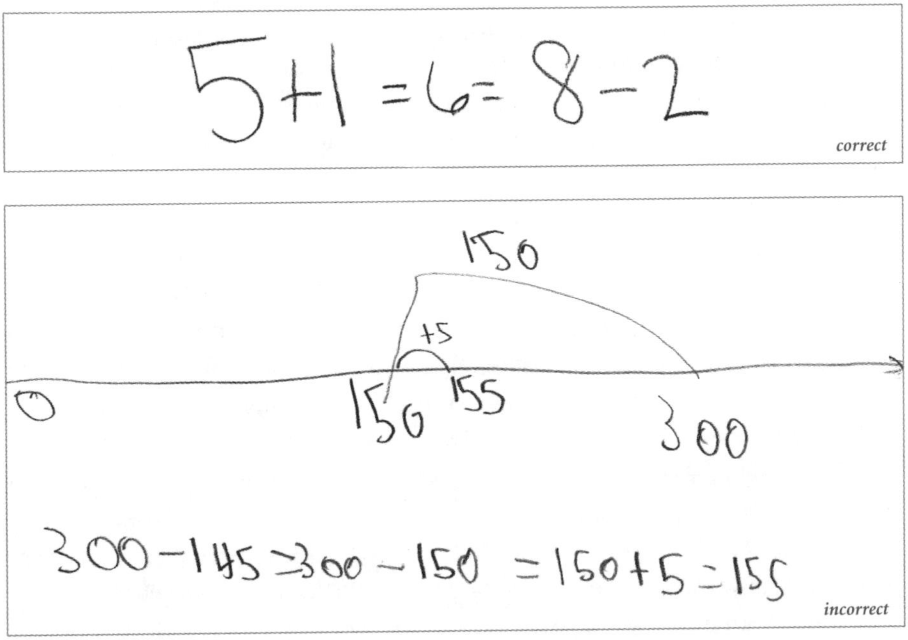

correct

incorrect

Figure 3.7
Correct and incorrect use of equals sign

Should we overlook the incorrect notation in the second example because one can follow the intent of the student's logic and the string of equations matches perceived movement on the number line? I know that I have been guilty of completely missing such an error when looking at student responses quickly. Other times I have chosen not to address the issue because another mathematical idea was the focus of a lesson and I didn't want to distract students. But if every teacher sidesteps this type of notation all of the time, when will students learn the correct and incorrect use of the equals sign? Similar to the tension we may feel in literacy learning between teaching the craft of writing and teaching writing conventions, we may be unsure of when to attend to getting math ideas on paper and when to pay attention to accuracy. You may wish to talk with your colleagues about this idea, too, to learn how they give adequate attention to accurate use of symbols without diminishing students' interest in communicating their mathematical ideas.

Math Vocabulary

"Learning math is like learning a new language. All languages have their own vocabulary, and mathematics is no exception" (Bruun, Diaz, and Dykes 2015; 536).Vocabulary is a tool that supports effective communication. Understanding what words mean helps students understand what is said, read, or written, as well as use a correct word or phrase in their own speaking or writing.

Focused vocabulary instruction is important for all students, and much has been written about why it is especially important for English language learners (ELLs). The growing number of ELLs in our classrooms makes it more necessary than ever for teachers to also think of themselves as teachers of language while they are teaching math. As you know, there is a difference between social and academic language. Cognitive Academic Language Proficiency can take five to seven years, or even longer, to achieve, as it focuses on the formal language used in academic settings. Part of that proficiency involves vocabulary acquisition, and math terms can be complicated, because several words have a slightly or completely different meaning in everyday life. For example, thinking of a *table* as a piece of furniture does not help a student understand a table as a way to organize information in rows and columns. Fortunately, we can sometimes build specific mathematical meaning from a word's everyday use. As fourth-grade teacher Carolyn Dwyer explained, "I help my students distinguish the terms *factors* and *products* from their knowledge that factories produce products."

Today, more than ever, students are exposed to, and expected to use, precise mathematical vocabulary. When using pattern blocks, we now refer to a rhombus rather than a diamond. Beginning in the primary grades, I hear students use terms such as *decompose* and *subitize*. Such vocabulary must emerge from the genuine explorations of ideas and build from more natural language such as *breaking apart*. Students need many opportunities to wrestle with what different words mean, and have many opportunities to use such terms. In her valuable 2017 NCSM Ignite talk, "Precision Over Perfect" (https://youtu.be/wc3yU5YNpwE), Christine Newell reminds us how important it is to let students lead the development of precise vocabulary.

To ensure that a lesson is accessible to all students, many teachers *always* preteach vocabulary at the beginning of a lesson. Although such an approach may often be beneficial, doing so sometimes keeps students from investigating mathematical ideas in ways that lead to conceptual understanding. For example, words such as *equal groups* or *array* may need to be previewed before an introductory lesson on multiplication, but *multiply* should be introduced at the end of the lesson, because beginning with its definition would be teaching by telling (Bay-Williams and Livers 2009). These authors also suggest that teachers limit review of vocabulary words to no more than five minutes and, when possible, to consider moving reviews to times outside of math class by including math terms in a question of the day, morning meeting; or homework prompt.

Elaborate! Condense!

In thinking about how often students are asked to expand writing or, alternatively, to write more concisely, I began to wonder how these same skills could help students better understand the language of mathematics, giving particular attention to the ideas math terms represent.

Mathematical language is often described as being dense. Think of how much information is contained in the simple statement $E = mc^2$. We can have students elaborate on mathematical meaning by exploring a single given sentence and recording all they know. You can offer this Elaborate! routine at the beginning of class or as part of your morning meeting message. Here are some possible prompts:

- Jeri is wearing more than 4 and fewer than 10 buttons.
- Daniel is taller than Jamal and shorter than Massie.
- Starting at 3:00 p.m., until the office closes at 5:00 p.m., appointments are available every fifteen minutes.
- The sum of the digits in the four-digit number is 8.
- The product of the digits in the three-digit number is 36.
- The area of the four-sided polygon is 18 square inches.
- The perimeter of the regular hexagon is 54 cm.
- Three buses were needed to take the 124 fifth graders to the science museum.

Mathematics supervisor Karen Gartland introduced an elaboration task to a group of third-grade students by saying, "Detectives need to think about the clues they find and make sure they are getting all the information they can from what they learn. We need to do this in math, too." She presented students with the sentence *The sum of the digits in the four-digit number is 8* and asked them to jot down what it told them—that is, to note the many ideas they could discover in this one sentence. Two examples of student thinking are shown in Figure 3.8. Notice how Skyler's response vacillates between specific examples and general ideas, both of which can help decipher the meaning of this sentence. Dana focuses on generalizations. She also expresses frustration at not having enough information to solve the problem.

Both Eli and Bethany were better prepared and more eager to solve the complete logic problem that followed:

> *The sum of the digits in the four-digit number is 8.*
> *You say the number when you count by tens.*
> *You do not say the number when you count by hundreds.*
> *The number is greater than 6,000.*

It was clear to Karen that focusing on the meaning of the first clue helped all of the students be more successful. She commented, "I appreciated how this activity helped students make implicit ideas explicit. Sometimes students think there is not enough information to solve a problem, when really, they just haven't recognized all of the information available to them."

Figure 3.8

Students' elaborations of <u>The sum of the digits in the four-digit number is 8.</u>

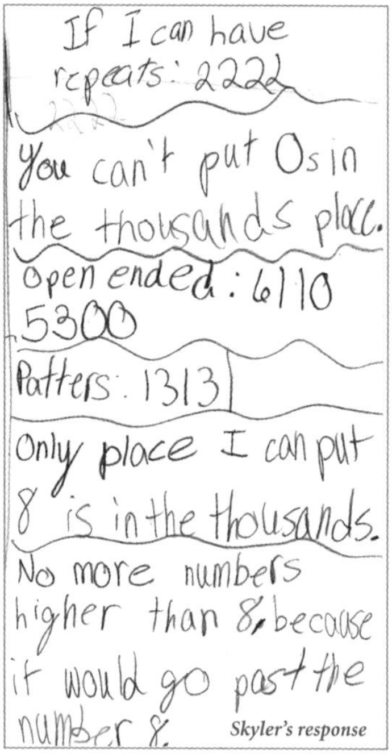

If I can have repeats: 2222
You can't put 0s in the thousands place.
Open ended: 6110
5300
Patters: 1313
Only place I can put 8 is in the thousands.
No more numbers higher than 8, because it would go past the number 8.

Skyler's response

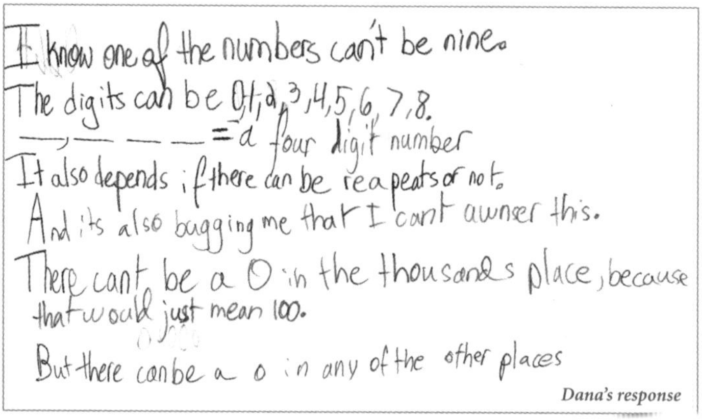

I know one of the numbers can't be nine.
The digits can be 0, 1, 2, 3, 4, 5, 6, 7, 8.
____ ____ ____ ____ = a four digit number
It also depends if there can be reapeats or not.
And its also bugging me that I can't awnser this.
There cant be a 0 in the thousands place, because that would just mean 100.
But there can be a 0 in any of the other places

Dana's response

Having students condense the clues in a logic problem can also deepen their focus on the meaning of the clues and the relationships among them. To focus on pattern finding and relationships among multiples, Karen gave a group of fourth-grade students, who had been exploring factors and multiples, the following logic problem and said, "Hmm, there are a lot of clues here. Do you think you could give this information in fewer sentences?" Before continuing to read, you might want to try this task yourself.

What could the number be?
It is a multiple of 2.
It is greater than 10.
It is an even number.
It is less than 100.
It is a multiple of 5.

Some students began by making notes about the clues. Several others focused on making a list of the numbers that would meet the clues, perhaps because they were used to solving similar problems, not thinking about the overlap among them. Karen offered the students a reminder, which helped to focus their thinking: "I see lots of good effort here toward solving the problem. But remember that this time, before you solve it, I asked you to try to give the information in fewer clues."

Oka's response is shown in Figure 3.9. Though he doesn't explicitly rewrite a condensed version of the clues, he does identify the relationships among multiples of 2, 5, and 10 and even numbers. He omits reference to the numbers being between 10 and 100. As he explained to Karen, "I could add that, but I wanted to focus on the stuff that could be eliminated." Note that he also lists the numbers that fit all of the clues.

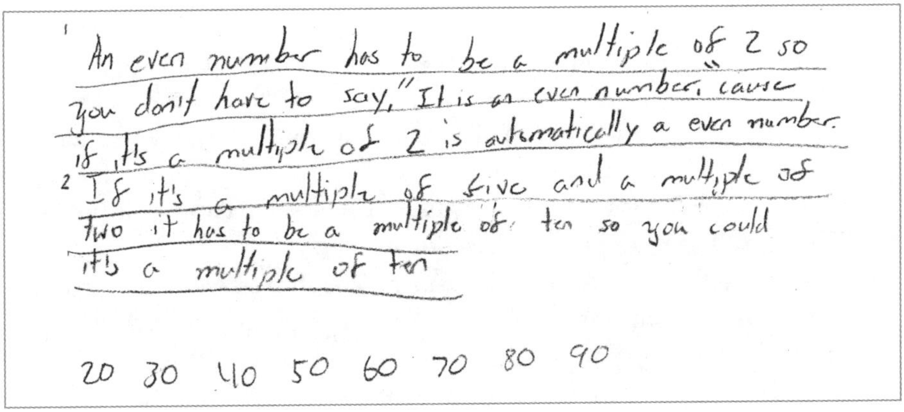

1 An even number has to be a multiple of 2 so you don't have to say, "It is an even number." cause if it's a multiple of 2 is automatically a even number.
2 If it's a multiple of five and a multiple of two it has to be a multiple of ten so you could it's a multiple of ten

20 30 40 50 60 70 80 90

Figure 3.9 Oka's response

Natalie recorded her initial ideas and then talked about them with Lucas. Through their discussion, they realized that the statements could be further condensed. It was great to hear Lucas exclaim, "Wow, I can't believe you can say so much with so little!" What a delightful comment to hear. One way students can simplify problem statements is to weed out information that is extraneous or redundant as they search for necessary data. Both students rewrote their ideas. Figure 3.10 shows Natalie's initial thoughts and her revision.

Figure 3.10
Natalie's response

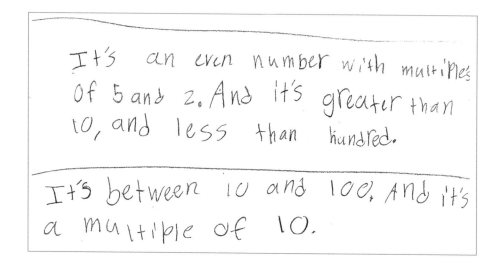

It's an even number with multiples of 5 and 2. And it's greater than 10, and less than hundred.

It's between 10 and 100. And it's a multiple of 10.

As a quick Condense! routine you can offer sentences such as the following and ask students to figure out why the second sentence is not needed or just ask them what they notice. You can also challenge upper-elementary students to create their own redundant sentences. To do so, some students elaborate on the first sentence, to figure out what they already know, and in doing so, discover one or two more unnecessary sentences they can include.

- I counted between 5 and 7 soccer balls. I counted an even number of soccer balls.
- Lisbeth added a number less than 4 to the number 5. She got a sum less than 9.
- Mike picked some roses and some daisies. He picked 3 daisies. He picked 4 flowers in all. He picked more daises than roses.
- Greta found the sum of two odd numbers. The sum was even.
- The two-digit number is a multiple of 9 and 3. The sum of the digits in the number is 9.
- The shape is a square. The shape is a rectangle.

In grades 3–5, elaborating is easier for some students; for some, condensing is easier. For K–1 students, condensing is more challenging, perhaps because they are just beginning to learn about mathematical relationships and academic language. Both of these routines provide ways for students to deepen their understanding of mathematical language and ideas. They also give students practice thinking about what specific math terms mean in an applied situation. As one fourth-grade student told me, "This makes me think differently. I hope I remember to think about what I learned about the math clues when I take a quiz."

Open-Ended Questions and Tasks

Asking students to write in response to open-ended questions and tasks provides opportunities for them to apply and further develop their knowledge of math vocabulary. *What do you know about . . .* is a simple prompt that can be used many times during the course of the year. All students can respond to this question, and responses can be updated as learning increases.

Toward the end of a unit on area and perimeter, mathematics specialist Kathy O'Connell Hopping showed fourth-grade students a picture of a shaded rectangle, listed that the side measures were 3 centimeters and 10 centimeters, and asked them to write everything they knew about the shape. The task is shown in Figure 3.11.

Name _____Date _____

What Do You know About....

One side is 3 centimeters and one side is 10 centimeters.

Write everything you know about this shape.

_____

_____

_____

_____

_____

_____

_____

Figure 3.11
Format of open-ended question

Marietta responded by making a list (Figure 3.12). Her work demonstrated that she could use a great many geometric terms correctly. She worked diligently, sometimes pausing and looking up between ideas, and then eagerly returning to her writing when she thought of something new to write. Observing her, you could sense that she was going to keep on listing facts until she couldn't think of anything else to write.

Figure 3.12
Marietta's response

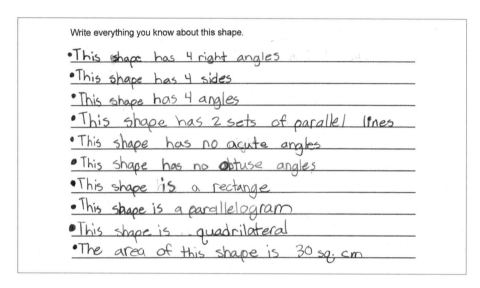

Write everything you know about this shape.

- This shape has 4 right angles
- This shape has 4 sides
- This shape has 4 angles
- This shape has 2 sets of parallel lines
- This shape has no acute angles
- This shape has no obtuse angles
- This shape is a rectange
- This shape is a parallelogram
- This shape is a quadrilateral
- The area of this shape is 30 sq. cm

Harry (Figure 3.13) used precise language that showed he had grasped many geometric terms and concepts. His narrative also correctly identified that if the shape were split in half, the area would also be half, but he then overgeneralized this relationship to perimeter. It reminded his teacher that many other students have that same misunderstanding. He also noted that he correctly calculated both the area and the perimeter, though he didn't use square units for the area. His response would be an excellent example to share with other students, because it combines unique ideas with thinking that needs revision.

Galina is a bilingual student who has received a diagnosis of a specific learning disability that affects reading, writing, and math. This format allowed her to identify several things she knew (Figure 3.14). Galina correctly identified the name of the shape, and though she used the more everyday term *corners*, wrote that the shape had four sides and four corners. The more precise term can be introduced and reinforced, and will be easier to learn now that she has identified the attribute. She noted that two sides are small and the other two sides are bigger, and repeated the given length measurements.

Many students wrote about some of the same ideas included in these three examples. Others also referenced the shape's lines of symmetry, referred to per-

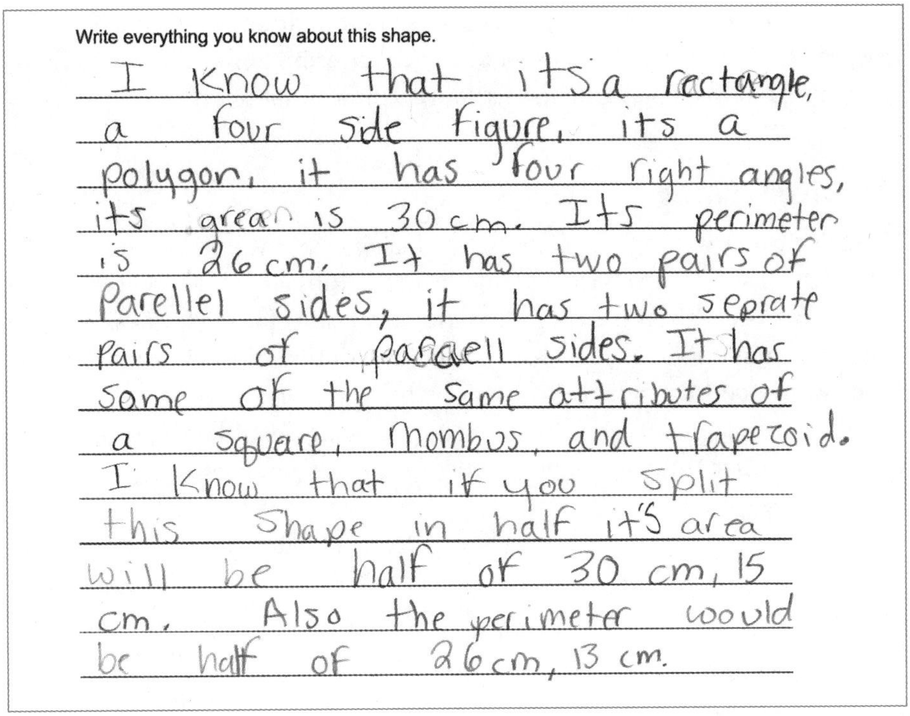

Write everything you know about this shape.

> I know that it's a rectangle, a four side figure, its a polygon, it has four right angles, its area is 30 cm. Its perimeter is 26 cm. It has two pairs of Parellel sides, it has two seprate pairs of paraell sides. It has some of the same attributes of a square, rhombus, and trapezoid. I know that if you split this shape in half it's area will be half of 30 cm, 15 cm. Also the perimeter would be half of 26 cm, 13 cm.

Figure 3.13
Harry's response

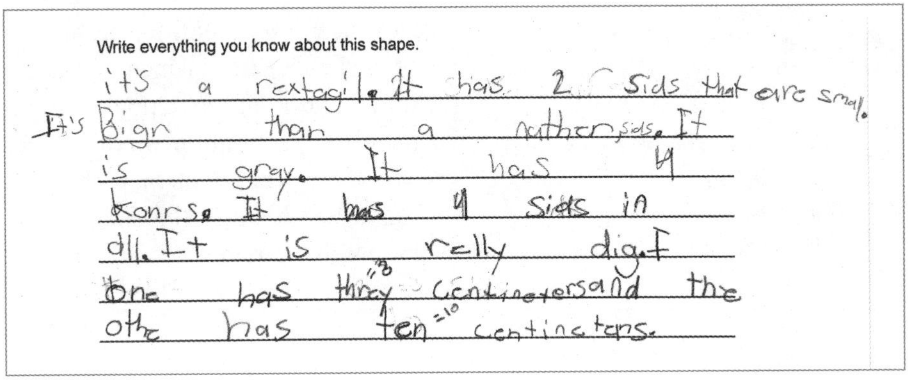

Write everything you know about this shape.

> It's a rextagile. It has 2 sids that are small. It's Bign than a nothensids. It is gray. It has 4 konrs. It has 4 sids in all. It is relly diqf. one has thiry "30" centimetersand the other has ten "10" centinctens.

Figure 3.14
Galina's response

pendicular lines, recorded the formulas used to find area and perimeter, and noted that the sum of the internal angles was 360 degrees. The variety of responses offered several opportunities for further vocabulary development. It also illustrated why open-ended activities serve all students well and that we need to be sure that every student is given opportunities to use writing to communicate mathematical ideas.

To further capitalize on this experience the next day, Kathy organized students in groups of four and asked them to try to identify *four math vocabulary words that you and other students included and one vocabulary word another student used that you did not include.* Here student writing served as a bridge to new learning. Such sharing is also a way to capture and honor everyone's ideas, something too challenging to do in a conversation about math.

Creative Writing

Though creative writing is a major focus of Chapter 8, I would like to note here that it can serve as a vehicle for supporting vocabulary development. Third grader Owen was given the choice to write definitions for *trapezoid* and *parallelogram* to put on the word wall; to write a description of what he would draw in the word-guessing game Pictionary for the word *polygon*; or to write a letter from one shape to another. By opening our thinking about how students write in math, we offer authentic opportunities to use math language.

Figure 3.15
Owen's letter

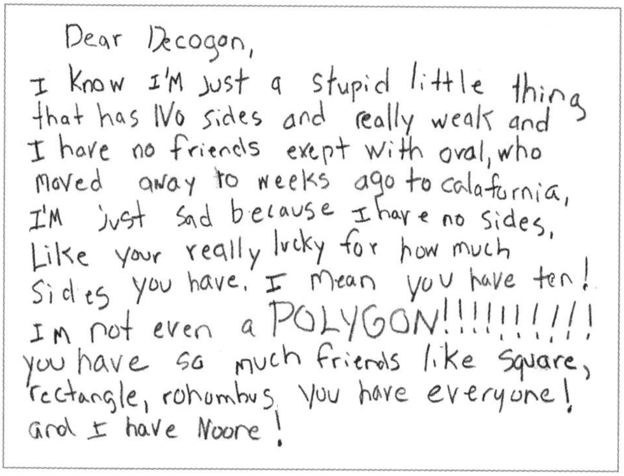

> Dear Decogon,
> I know I'M just a stupid little thing that has IVo sides and really weak and I have no friends exept with oval, who moved away two weeks ago to calafornia, I'M just sad because I have no sides, Like your really lucky for how much Sides you have. I mean you have ten! I'M not even a POLYGON!!!!!!!!//| you have so much friends like Square, rectangle, rohombus, you have everyone! and I have Noone!

Owen chose to write a letter to a decagon. In his response (Figure 3.15) he made connections to themes in *The Greedy Triangle* (Burns 1994) and to the rigidity of a triangle that he learned about in a STEM lesson. His author's voice is clear. He never identifies the author of the letter, Circle, which makes me think about the potential of students writing anonymous letters and then posting them so that all can try to identify the shapes who have written them.

Next Steps

Writing with and about numbers, symbols, and words can help students clarify thinking and provide teachers with important insights. Though it's essential to teach about numbers, symbols, and math vocabulary to support students' mathematical language, we need to think in much broader terms (Moschkovich 2012). Becoming language proficient means much more than learning the precise meaning of technical words and symbols. Students must also learn what mathematical explorations, explanations, and reasoning look like and what it means to describe or justify their thinking. These ideas will be explored in the next few chapters.

4 Writing to Explore

Exploratory writing—which can include brainstorming, taking notes, making representations, finding patterns, and probing ideas—can be a wonderful way for students to engage in a math problem or task. Through exploratory writing, students document their initial thinking and note possible pathways for further exploration. Exploratory writing can lead to an exciting adventure into the unknown.

Writing to Discover Meaning: Story Problems

When students are given a problem to solve, they might make a drawing or jot notes to represent the situation. As they do so, they are using writing as a way to make sense. During a snowy week in January, Becky Eston Salemi asked her kindergarten students to consider the following question: *If everyone in your family had a pair of mittens, how many mittens would there be?* These young learners needed time to think about this question. They needed to consider the size of their families and how many mittens each member would need. Then they had to decide how they could represent this situation to keep track of all those people and mittens. As they worked, they were writing not to *show how*

Figure 4.1
Three examples of student work

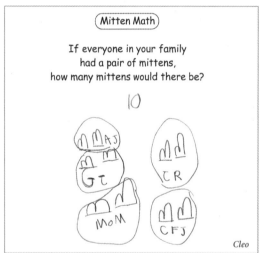

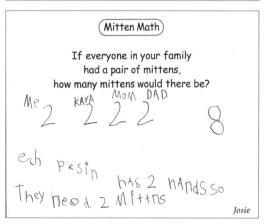

they got their answers, but to *make sense of the information*, so they could understand the task. Three examples of student work are shown in Figure 4.1.

From just these three responses, we see very different levels of thinking. Trevor's response is similar to where many students begin, showing all the information in a picture. While drawing, Trevor turned to his neighbor and said, "This is my dog, Arlo. He needs four mittens." Once he completed his representation, he focused on counting the total number of mittens he had drawn.

Cleo's work shows a more abstract representation of the people in her family. She drew a pair of mittens for each family member and a circle around each pair, and then added initials (with the exception of her label *Mom*) to identify which family member was indicated. Josie's response is even more abstract. She wrote the names of each family member and then *2* below each name, allowing for the possibility of counting by twos. Once Josie completed her exploratory writing, she provided a justification for her thinking by writing about the relationship between the number of hands and the number of mittens each person had.

When the students shared their individual thinking with the group, questions such as *What do you notice about the different ways you have represented the people in your family? What do you suppose these letters mean?* and *What do the 2s mean?* bring attention to the different ways of exploring these ideas and provide students with a variety of ways to make information in a problem meaningful.

Such notations change over time and allow us to capture growth in thinking. During a rainy week in April, Becky posed the same problem again, but in the context of rain boots. Trevor (Figure 4.2) drew pairs of legs with boots and then recorded the number of people and boots above his representation. This time, he did not include his dog.

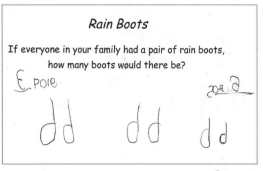

Rain Boots

If everyone in your family had a pair of rain boots, how many boots would there be?

Rich problems offer students of all ages a reason to explore their thinking through writing. Math specialist Kathy O'Connell Hopping was working with a group of four

Figure 4.2
Trevor's response

third graders who were having difficulty with word problems. As she watched them work, she realized that all of them were automatically underlining nearly everything in the problem statement. She said they were underlining so quickly, she couldn't even be sure they were reading the words first. To slow them down, she asked them to rewrite (using words and drawings) the information in the problem they thought was important. *Write and draw first* became their mantra.

Kathy and these four students had been working together for several weeks when she asked them to solve the following multistep problem. Too often we oversimplify problems, which deprives students of the opportunity to experience productive struggle. Kathy wanted them to appreciate how writing and drawing helped them make sense of the problem.

> *This morning, Nick made some blueberry muffins.*
> *His mom took 2 dozen of them to her meeting.*
> *His sister ate 2 of them.*
> *His dad took 6 of the muffins to his grandmother.*
> *Nick put the last 4 muffins in a bag and wrote "MINE" on it.*
> *How many muffins did Nick make this morning?*

Consider Maddie's work shown in Figure 4.3. Notice the bulleted list of facts, which she then illustrated to make this information more meaningful. Once she explored the problem in this way, she went back to read the question. She then said, "Oh, I get it. I just put them together. I think this draw-and-write thing is working out for me." Kathy said it seemed as if Maddie could let go of the first five lines of text once she knew she had captured them in her exploratory writing. That meant she could just concentrate on the question, which was clearer to her now that all of the muffins were represented on her paper. She quickly wrote her equation and labeled her answer.

Figure 4.3
Maddie's
exploratory
notes and
drawings

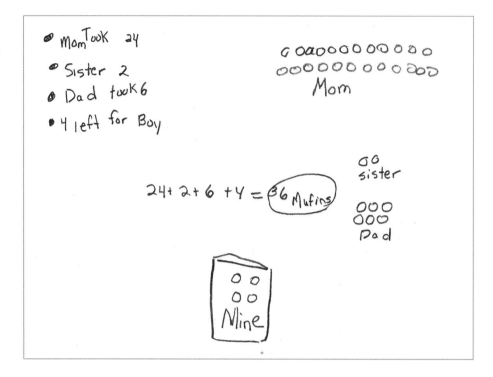

Routines

In recent years, many online resources, and particularly the Math Twitter Blogosphere, have given mathematics educators access to numerous resources and routines that support the exploration of mathematical ideas. Questions such as *What do you notice? What do you wonder?* are often embedded in these routines. These questions were popularized by Suzanne Alejandre, Annie Fetter, and Max Ray-Riek, folks at the Math Forum, a powerful online resource within the National Council of Teachers of Mathematics. Noticing and wondering provide a way to activate students' thinking and offer opportunities for them to make sense of mathematical situations and pose questions. They are also excellent entry points into writing, because everyone can notice something, and recording students' thinking makes these routines more powerful.

One example of a routine that supports exploratory thinking is a simple puzzle that presents four numbers, shapes, objects, or graphs and asks, *Which one doesn't belong?* Christopher Danielson (@Trianglemancsd), a member of the teaching faculty at Desmos, which creates digital tools for learning math and makes them available on the Internet, has written a book of which-one-doesn't-belong (wodb) puzzles focused on shapes (Danielson 2016). A variety of number, shape, and data wodb puzzles can also be found at http://wodb.ca/. I think of wodb as a focused *What do you notice?* question. An example is given in Figure 4.4. You may want to consider what your response would be before reading further.

I presented this wodb fraction task shown in Figure 4.4 to a class of fourth graders. I began by asking them to look at the pictures and silently decide which one didn't belong. I waited for about twenty seconds and then invited them to turn and talk with a partner. I could also have begun by simply asking what they noticed or which ones they thought went together.

Figure 4.4
Fraction
Which one
doesn't
belong?

After a short time, I asked students to share their ideas with the class as I recorded their thinking (Figure 4.5). As with number talks, this shared writing is an important aspect of the routine, even though it is not the students who are doing the recording. Such summaries can help remind students what was discussed as well as be a way to celebrate student thinking. I ended the routine by

Figure 4.5
Annotated
which one
doesn't
belong?

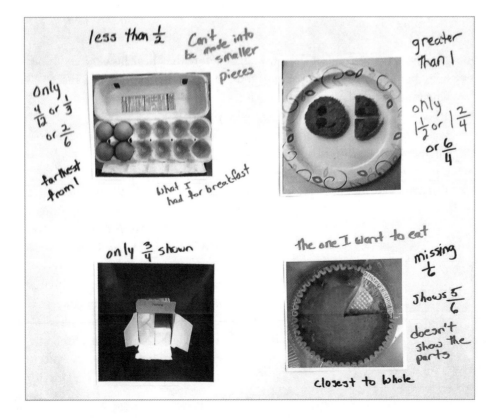

saying, "I'm going to leave this posted here, so you can continue to look at it throughout the day and perhaps add some new ideas. Then you can come back to it before you leave today and find out what else you mathematicians have been discovering."

It is delightful to offer a wodb task to students who have never seen one. At first, I find that they are satisfied with their initial responses and are therefore surprised to learn that their peers have other ideas. When they realize that a variety of responses are possible, I often see shoulders relax, eyes widen, and attention increase—as if students have been given an invitation to succeed. It is a wonderful moment.

These students had just completed a couple of lessons on equivalent fractions, so I was not surprised that several such fractions were identified early in the discussion. I had intentionally included a picture that showed less than one-half and one that showed a quantity greater than one, because the next topic of study was comparing fractions with benchmark numbers. It was only after names of fractions were identified that students' comments focused on comparative relationships. I was struck by the comment that one of the pictures didn't "show the parts." Do we show students enough of such images?

It's often helpful to students to jot down some ideas before they talk with others. Doing so can:

◦ give them time to collect their thoughts before they hear how others think;
◦ help them persevere, because they tend to be more accepting of pauses when they write than when they talk;
◦ rehearse ideas before sharing them with others;
◦ remember all of their ideas, which is particularly important when exploring many possibilities;
◦ reinforce the expectation of multiple ideas; and
◦ stimulate new ideas when thinking is reread or shared with a partner.

Figure 4.6
Which one doesn't belong? problem offered to first graders

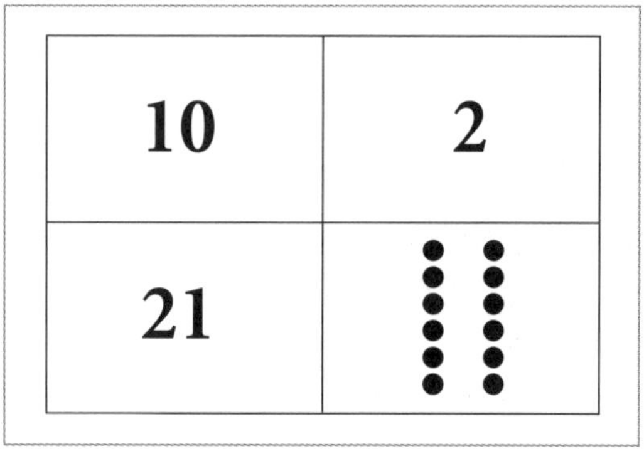

Math specialist Karen Gartland presented the wodb task in Figure 4.6 to a group of first graders and asked them to record their thinking. Once they did so, she invited them to share their ideas with a partner.

Some students wrote about one possibility, some two. Figure 4.7 shows three students' responses. These students found different numbers or different reasons for their choices.

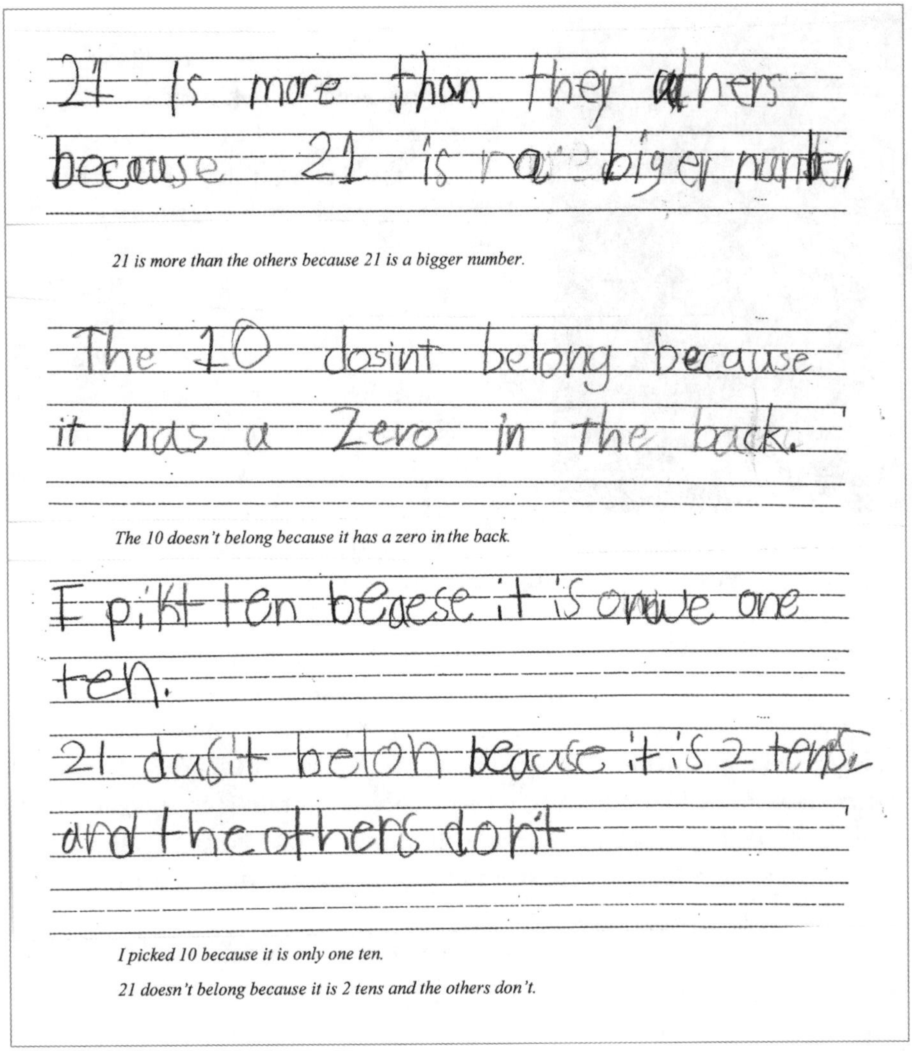

Figure 4.7
Three
students'
responses

> 21 Is more than they others
> because 21 is ra bigey number

21 is more than the others because 21 is a bigger number.

> The 10 dosint belong because
> it has a Zero in the back.

The 10 doesn't belong because it has a zero in the back.

> I pikt ten beaese it is onue one
> ten.
> 21 dusit beton beause it is 2 tens
> and the others don't

I picked 10 because it is only one ten.
21 doesn't belong because it is 2 tens and the others don't.

Writing to Remember: Finding Patterns

Mark Chubb is an instructional coach in Niagara, Canada. When his daughter was six years old, they used dice to create a pattern together (Figure 4.8). Mark shared it on Twitter (@MarkChubb3) and gave me permission to include it here. Patterns provide a wonderful opportunity for students to explore a variety of ideas. Have some fun. Stop reading and spend a few minutes noticing patterns. Challenge yourself to find at least five. Don't write anything down, but do put out a finger for each pattern you discover. Then keep your fingers where they are and continue to read.

Figure 4.8
Dice pattern

Look at your fingers. Can you identify the patterns they represent or, like many of us, do you need to look back at the image and rediscover several of them? If you had taken notes, you might have had to look at the dice again to remind yourself of the meaning of a particular phrase or two, but you would have been on much firmer ground. Whether created by jotting ideas down quickly or in such a way that someone else could follow our thinking, recording ideas is helpful. You may want to try the activity again, but this time write down the patterns you find. Then ask yourself if you have provided enough details to easily find each pattern. When I've shared this task with teachers, nearly all of them have come up with more ideas, and described them more specifically, when recording is included. I can't tell you that writing down their thoughts increased their ability to find patterns, but I can tell you that they spent more time looking for patterns when they recorded what they found. Perhaps their minds were free to look for a different pattern once the previous one was safely noted. Figure 4.9 shows an example of a list I made. I felt fairly solid until a group of teachers pointed out that there were patterns within the color of the pips (the dots on the dice), that there was a line of symmetry, that all of the dice with a 1 on them were pink or maroon and . . . !

There is much to discover in this dice image; the picture is worthy of exploration at multiple grade levels. Students in the upper-elementary grades can make lists similar to the one I made.

In a second-grade classroom, students gathered in the rug area and viewed the dice image on a screen. Math specialist Kathy O'Connell Hopping asked them to independently look for patterns and record their ideas on their whiteboards (Figure 4.10). Then they shared their findings. As they did so, she asked the class questions such as *Does what you've heard let you see this pattern?* and *Who can restate what was just said?* The term *diagonal* came up and was reviewed, and students gradually learned to be more specific.

Kathy then asked the students to work in pairs to find more patterns. She gave them a recording sheet to share and told them that they would each write down two patterns. The students were asked to write in a way that would allow them to quickly find the patterns once again. Though required to each write about only two, several students turned over their papers and continued to

1) Color at end and beginning of each row is the same.

2) Color at top and bottom of each column is the same.

3) Numbers on diagonals going left-to-right (down) are the same.

4) Numbers on right-to-left (down) diagonals alternate: all odd, all even...

5) Numbers in rows continuously repeat 1-6.

6) Starting at lower right column and going up, then down to next colum, numbers repeat 1-6.

7) Going left to right (down), first and last numbers on diagonals are the same.

8) Going right to left (down), first and last numbers sum to 8, (when there are at least two number.).

9) Sums of rows increase by one, starting at 15 for the first row and ending at 19 for the last row.

10) Sums of columns decrease by one, starting at 19 for the left-most column, and ending at 15 for the right-most column.

11) Sums of the top and bottom numbers in each of the first four columns increase by 2, starting on the left: 4, 6, 8, 10

12) The same sums described in #11 can be found by adding first and last numbers in each row, starting at the bottom.

Figure 4.9
My initial
list of
patterns

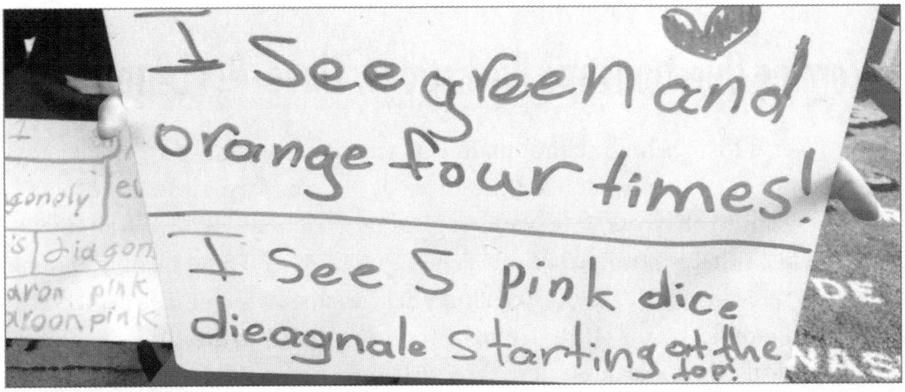

I See green and orange four times!

I see 5 pink dice dieagnale starting at the top!

Figure 4.10
Response
recorded on
whiteboard
(note that
these
students
refer to the
yellow/lime
green dice
as green)

Figure 4.11
Recording
sheet for
patterns

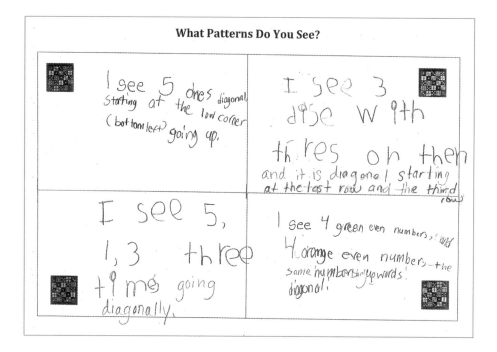

What Patterns Do You See?

I see 5 ones diagonal starting at the low corner (bottom left) going up.

I see 3 dise with thres oh then and it is diagonal starting at the last row and the third row

I see 5, 1, 3 three time going diagonally.

I see 4 green even numbers, and 4 orange even numbers—the same number the up words! diagonal.

record patterns they identified. A response is shown in Figure 4.11. I'm uncertain whether these students were unclear on directionality, or rotated the figure.

Note that an adult has recorded some additional information on the response sheet. This student receives support when writing is involved. Once the student identified a pattern, the assistant asked him to tell her more about it, to help clarify where the pattern was. The assistant acted as a scribe, recording only words that the student said. As this activity moved from students recording patterns so they could remember them to writing more specifically so they could find them quickly, they included aspects of descriptive writing, which we'll explore further in the next chapter.

Recording Questions and Predictions: Three-Act Lessons

Dan Meyer, a former high school math teacher who is serving as the chief academic officer at Desmos, created the three-act lesson format. In his May 11, 2013, blog entry, he wrote, "Storytelling gives us a framework for certain mathematical tasks that is both prescriptive enough to be *useful* and flexible enough to be *usable.* Many stories divide into three acts, each of which maps neatly onto these mathematical tasks" (http://blog.mrmeyer.com/2011/the-three-acts-of-a-mathematical-story). Each of these three acts serves a specific purpose.

Act 1: Students are shown a brief visual prompt that stimulates their curiosity.
Act 2: Students consider information and tools they need to investigate the situation further. And, once students discuss what is needed, they are usually provided with more information.
Act 3: Students draw conclusions, and a new story line may be initiated.

Math specialist Graham Fletcher has been particularly active in the creation of three-act lessons appropriate for elementary school students. Several of his tasks can be found at https://gfletchy.com/. As suggested in Fletcher's "All Aboard" three-act lesson, Karen Gartland showed a third-grade class a video clip of a locomotive passing a railroad crossing. She then told them they were going to watch the video again and that this time they should start noticing what they saw. When they shared what they noticed, comments included, *There were lots of train cars, The train was moving really fast,* and *I think I saw two engines.*

Students were then asked to discuss what they wondered. Comments included, *Why is the car going by? Why is there writing on the train cars?* and *Why are there all those lights?* Karen asked them to record the questions they might explore. Once it was decided that the group would focus on the question *How long does it take all of the cars to pass?* students also made estimates to predict their answers. An example of a student's recording can be found in Figure 4.12.

Having explored initial ideas, chosen a question, and made estimates, the students were ready for act 2. Consider the teacher's reflection on this lesson format.

Figure 4.12 Sample student recording

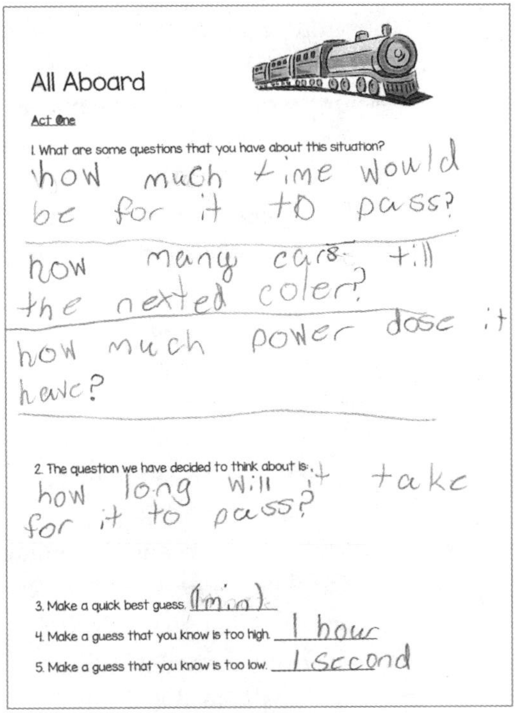
All Aboard

Act One

1. What are some questions that you have about this situation?
how much time would be for it to pass?
how many cars till the nexted coler?
how much power dose it have?

2. The question we have decided to think about is: how long will it take for it to pass?

3. Make a quick best guess. (1min)
4. Make a guess that you know is too high. 1 hour
5. Make a guess that you know is too low. 1 second

Karen's Reflection

I really like the format of a three-act lesson. It is often a great way to introduce or reinforce a standard that I am teaching. It amazes me how many examples are available online for free. The videos capture my students' attention, and I really appreciate what happens when they explore possibilities. Often their initial brainstorming includes many ideas not related to math, but when they write down their questions and exchange them, they almost always become more focused on math-related questions.

I also like to see their recorded estimates once we have chosen a question to pursue. Many of my students were way off in their estimates of time. Many "best estimates" were more than thirty minutes. It made me wonder if they have ever been in a car that was stopped while a train crossed. If the students hadn't written their estimates, I wouldn't have seen how widespread this misconception was. There are almost always a few students who are motivated to explore a related question after one of these lessons. This time a small group wanted to do some research on the usual length and weight of a train car.

Exploring New Thinking by Looking at Others' Writing

A few years ago, I wrote some tasks involving students drawing maps related to fractions (Dacey 2012). Their responses helped me gain an appreciation of the need for them to have many opportunities to think about fractions in a real-world context, rather than merely on number lines. Below is a similar task I wrote and the students in Donna Blake's fourth-grade class considered. Asking for a map could be replaced with the more open question *What do you know?* Or, students could respond to the more open question first and then draw a map. Any of these approaches is fine.

> *Jazmine lives on Main Street, 1 mile from school. Jazmine walks to school every day. When she is $\frac{1}{2}$ of a mile from home, she passes the post office. When she is $\frac{3}{4}$ of a mile from home, she passes the fire station. When she is $\frac{1}{8}$ of a mile from school, she passes Mia's house. Make a map to show your information.*

As the students began, Donna noticed little chatter in the room but lots of reading, rereading, drawing, and labeling. As she walked about, she saw that several students had begun by drawing a line. Sean's work caught her attention; rather than labeling the buildings on the map, he was creating a key (Figure 4.13). She appreciated that Sean had made a connection to their earlier work in social studies.

Donna noted that Emma had begun by making a list of essential information as she read and reread the problem. She observed a bit longer as Emma

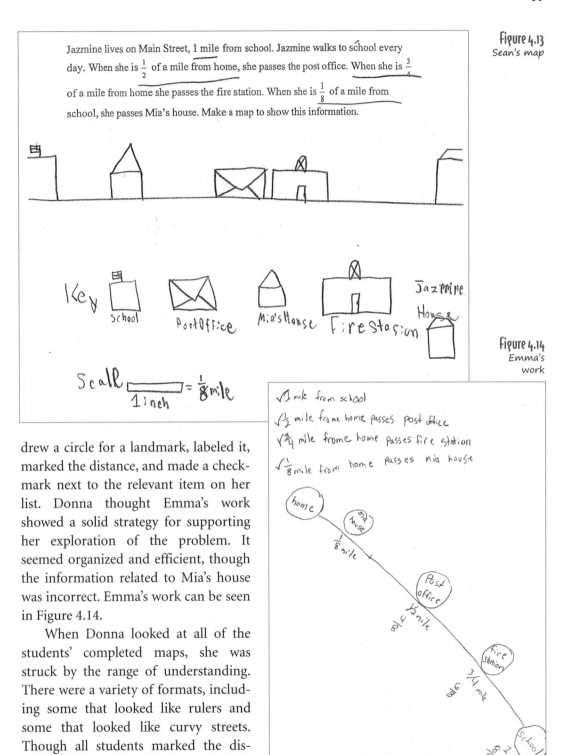

Figure 4.13
Sean's map

The figure contains the following text:

Jazmine lives on Main Street, 1 mile from school. Jazmine walks to school every day. When she is $\frac{1}{2}$ of a mile from home, she passes the post office. When she is $\frac{3}{4}$ of a mile from home she passes the fire station. When she is $\frac{1}{8}$ of a mile from school, she passes Mia's house. Make a map to show this information.

Key — School — Post Office — Mia's House — Fire Stasion — Jazmine House

Scale | 1 inch = $\frac{1}{8}$ mile

Figure 4.14
Emma's
work

✓ 1 mile from school
✓ $\frac{1}{2}$ mile frome home passes post office
✓ $\frac{3}{4}$ mile frome home passes fire station
✓ $\frac{1}{8}$ mile from home passes mia house

home — mia house — $\frac{1}{8}$ mile — Post office — $\frac{1}{2}$ mile — fire Station — $\frac{3}{4}$ mile — School — 1 mi

drew a circle for a landmark, labeled it, marked the distance, and made a checkmark next to the relevant item on her list. Donna thought Emma's work showed a solid strategy for supporting her exploration of the problem. It seemed organized and efficient, though the information related to Mia's house was incorrect. Emma's work can be seen in Figure 4.14.

When Donna looked at all of the students' completed maps, she was struck by the range of understanding. There were a variety of formats, including some that looked like rulers and some that looked like curvy streets. Though all students marked the distances, not everyone made proportional

Figure 4.15
Nonpropor-
tional map

drawings (Figure 4.15). She decided to take advantage of their earlier experience with writing comments about another student's work, instead of just sharing their own process and solutions. She knew that when her students were
asked to provide comments or advice, it helped them slow down and encouraged them to think more deeply as they continued to explore the task.

The next day Donna returned the students' responses and gave each student
a copy of another student's work. She also invited Maureen O'Connell, the
school's math specialist, to join the class. Donna explained to the students that
they were to read and comment on the other students' work and suggested they
might want to reread their own response as well. She said that both she and Ms.
O'Connell would be available to talk.

Emma had a copy of Sean's work. She placed the two responses side by side
and began to turn Sean's paper sideways and upside down. She then brought
both responses to Maureen at the back table, where they had the following conversation. Before reading this dialogue, you may want to review Emma's and
Sean's responses and note that along with somewhat different representational
styles, they oriented the school at different ends of their maps and didn't place
all the landmarks in the same places. As you read this conversation, notice how
pauses allowed the student to stay focused on her own thoughts and to continue to develop her ideas.

Emma: It's backward.
Maureen: What do you mean?
Emma: He starts at school and ends at home.
Maureen: Can you say more?
Emma: See (*pointing to the school*), his is here and I have Jazmine's
house there. (*She draws her finger across her map from left to right.*)
Wait, maybe it doesn't matter.
Maureen: What do you mean?
Emma: Well, I guess it goes from here to there or from there to here.
(*She draws her finger across her map from left to right and then on
Sean's from right to left.*)

There is a pause.

Emma: No. Something's really not right. I have the fire station halfway
between the post office and the school, but Sean has placed it right
next to the post office and closer to Jazmine's house.

There is another pause.

Emma: Oh no, Mia's house is not right either.
Maureen: What do you think is wrong?
Emma: Mia's house is $\frac{1}{8}$ of a mile from her house, but Sean has it $\frac{1}{8}$ of a
mile from school. Look, you can see his scale. (*Emma points to the
scale Sean has included on his sheet where he recorded* 1 inch $= \frac{1}{8}$
mile.) Which one is right?
Maureen: How can you decide?

Emma rereads the problem on Sean's paper. She notices that he has under-
lined some key information and reports, "It says, *When she is $\frac{1}{8}$ of a mile from
school.* Oh, now I see." She then goes back to her work area, changes her fourth
listed fact, and erases Mia's house from her map (Figure 4.16). She relocates it
by finding where she believes $\frac{1}{8}$ of a mile should be.

Emma returns her attention to Sean's map and draws an arrow where she
thinks the fire station should be. Then, because she was asked to provide a comment, she also offers Sean words of advice (Figure 4.17).

A few other students wanted to talk through their thinking with Donna or
Maureen, but several worked directly with their partners. Overall, Donna and
Maureen were impressed with how much more closely the students paid atten-
tion to comparing responses when they had a copy of each other's work and the

Figure 4.16
Emma's
edited work

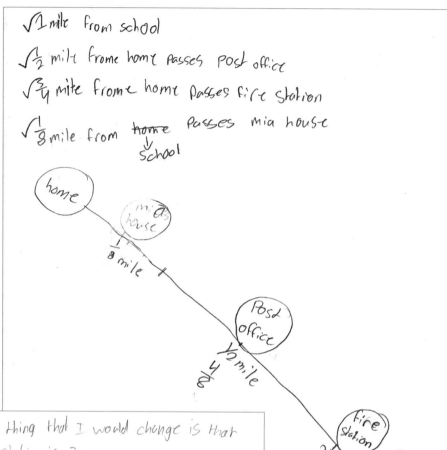

√ 1 mile from school

√ ½ mile frome home passes post office

√ ¾ mile frome home passes fire station

√ ⅛ mile from ~~home~~ passes mia house
                          ↓
                       school

Figure 4.17
Emma's
feedback to
Sean

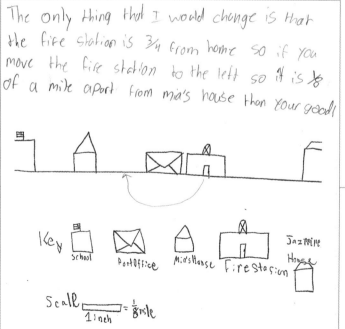

The only thing that I would change is that the fire station is ¾ from home so if you move the fire station to the left so it is ⅛ of a mile apart from mia's house than your good!

Key

School   PostOffice   Mia'sHouse   FireStation   Jazmine House

Scale ▭ = ⅛ mile
      1 inch

responsibility of creating a written response. Maureen commented, "When students just talk about their work, they jump right in, without necessarily reading each other's work carefully. This process seemed to slow them down and allowed them to attend to more details."

Writing to Keep Track of Findings: Investigations

There is no classroom activity I enjoy seeing more than students being actively involved in an investigation. Whether I watch kindergartners discovering all the combinations of eight, second graders figuring out how many seeds are in a pumpkin, or third graders finding different perimeters of rectangles for a given area, I am always reminded that this is the level of engagement I want students to experience all day long. One of the key aspects of such an investigation is the recording students do to keep track of their findings.

Math specialist Kathy O'Connell Hopping gave a group of fifth-grade students the following task to investigate:

> *Roll the two dice.*
> *Use each number rolled to create two two-digit numbers.*
> *Find their difference.*
> *Repeat several times.*
> *What happens?*

This task is also worth exploring before you continue to read. Feel free to just choose numbers if dice are not handy. For example, if the numbers were 3 and 6, you have 63 − 36 = 27.

Kathy wanted students to capture their thinking as they pursued the task, so she gave them the recording sheet shown in Figure 4.18 with the column headings *Subtraction Problem, What do you notice?* and *What are you wondering? Thinking?* She encouraged students to draw a line through the first noticing and wondering areas on their sheets, because they would have only one piece of information at that point.

Figure 4.18
Recording sheet for investigation

Subtraction Problem	What do you notice?	What are you wondering? Thinking?

Kathy distributed dice with the numbers 0–9 as well as the recording sheets, and students were eager to begin. They rolled individually, but as they began to notice patterns, they often turned to a neighbor to see if he or she had made the same observation. Initially the students saw the task as a simple one; however, once they started to notice patterns and raise questions, they became increasingly excited. Their voices rose as they began making discoveries and asking questions such as *Hey, are you getting multiples of three?* They never forgot to record their subtraction problems; they never had to be reminded to record what they noticed and wondered. They were involved, and eager to explore further. (See Figure 4.19.)

Figure 4.19
Students collecting and comparing data

Aiden's sheet (Figure 4.20) almost looks as if he is recording a running conversation with himself as he notices something, wonders about it, and then draws a conclusion. Like many students, he noticed what happened when the same number was rolled on each die. Don't you love his note in the lower-left corner where he wrote *Faked number to prove something,* to disclose that he created an example without rolling?

Having completed this page, Aiden looked up and said, "What about three-digit numbers?" This question motivated him so much that he turned over his paper and began to consider relevant examples (Figure 4.21). Other students explored new ideas as well, such as *What happens when you use six-sided dice?*

Figure 4.20
Aiden's
recording
sheet

What Do You Notice?

Roll 2 dice.
Create the largest number and the smallest number.
Subtract the smallest number from the largest number.

Subtraction Problem	What do you notice?	What are you wondering? Thinking?
$\begin{array}{r}{\scriptstyle 3}\,{\scriptstyle 4}\,{\scriptstyle \cancel{0}}^{10}\\ -\ 0\ 4\\ \hline 3\ 6\end{array}$		
$\begin{array}{r}{\scriptstyle 7}\,{\scriptstyle 8}\,{\scriptstyle \cancel{0}}^{10}\\ -\ \ 0\ 8\\ \hline 7\ 2\end{array}$	If you get 1 zero, the difference will be <10.	Always have to trade first
$\begin{array}{r}{\scriptstyle 2}\,{\scriptstyle \cancel{3}}\,{\scriptstyle \cancel{1}}^{11}\\ -\ 1\ 3\\ \hline 1\ 8\end{array}$	I do in fact always have to trade.	Difference will always be larger than the subtracting number?
$\begin{array}{r}{\scriptstyle 7}\,{\scriptstyle \cancel{8}}\,{\scriptstyle \cancel{6}}^{16}\\ -\ \ 6\ 8\\ \hline 1\ 8\end{array}$	Difference can be less	$\begin{array}{l}86 \to 68 \\ 83 \to 38\end{array}$ } how often?
$\begin{array}{r}{\scriptstyle 6}\,{\scriptstyle 7}\,{\scriptstyle \cancel{0}}^{10}\\ -\ \ 0\ 7\\ \hline 6\ 3\end{array}$	70→? If you decrease the 10s digit of the subtracted number you decrease the 60-26 1's by the same digit and vice versa.	how will this change with a 3 digit number!
$\begin{array}{r}{\scriptstyle 8}\,{\scriptstyle \cancel{4}}\,{\scriptstyle \cancel{6}}^{16}\\ -\ \ 6\ 9\\ \hline 2\ 7\end{array}$	You must trade with this strategy otherwise you will get it wrong.	Is it possible not to trade
faked number to prove something $\begin{array}{r}8\ 8\\ -\ 8\ 8\\ \hline 0\end{array}$	You do not trade if both digits are the same	What about zeros?

Which difference is most common? Posing their own questions is an important part of problem solving; in the real world, problems don't come to us well defined and written in a textbook!

Several students recorded comments in the wondering column that illustrated the intensity of their curiosity. Two examples are shown in Figure 4.22. The students remained engaged throughout their math period and asked if they could continue the next day. Kathy agreed, and with the extended time, their work focused on making claims and trying to prove them. In this way, their work moved organically from writing to explore to writing to stake a claim and defend it, that is, argumentative writing.

Figure 4.21
Exploration
of a new,
related
question

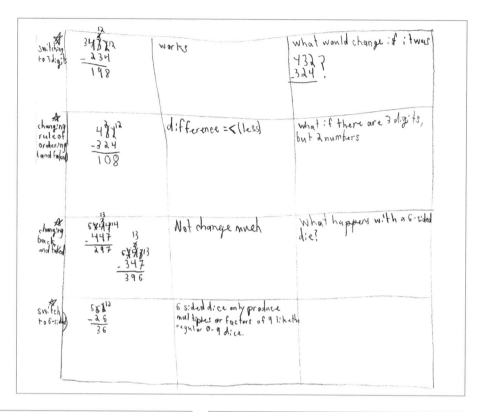

Figure 4.22
Examples of
written
comments
that express
curiosity

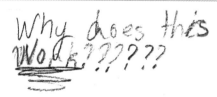

Closing Thoughts

Adding exploratory writing to a task that has numerous possibilities supports wonderful mathematical thinking. Here, I've suggested just a few of the routines and lesson formats that encourage this type of writing. Teachers can suggest structured response forms or students can write freestyle. Exploratory writing can also lead to students' creation of descriptive, explanatory, or argumentative pieces of work. What is important is that once engaged, students write because they want to write; they want to keep track of their ideas and discoveries. This is very different from writing for others. As other forms of writing are considered in next chapters, you will see that they can kindle this same level of energy.

5 Writing to Describe and Explain

aulo is asked to write to a younger student about something he thinks is important about division. He chooses to explain the usefulness of the relationship between multiplication and division. He writes about a specific example (Figure 5.1) and the general question to ask when trying to identify a missing factor.

Paulo's response is an example of explanatory writing: writing to describe and explain. This type of writing helps students develop mathematical language, solidify their thinking, and make connections. The focus here is on telling or describing *what* or *how*. Details and examples are important, because they help both the reader and the writer better visualize or understand the ideas being communicated. As you'll see later in the chapter, explanatory writing can also help develop students' awareness of how important quantitative details can be.

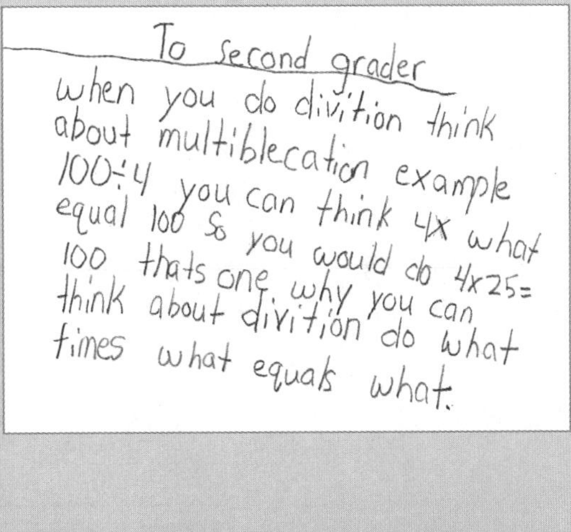

To second grader

when you do divition think about multiblecation example 100÷4 you can think 4x what equal 100 So you would do 4x25= 100 thats one why you can think about divition do what times what equals what.

Figure 5.1
Paulo's letter about division

How to Solve a Problem

When students explain their thinking to us, we are given a glimpse into how their minds work. It is a gift, an act of trust that holds invaluable instructional potential. Written explanations are another way to gain access to student thinking. In fact, this type of writing may be the most common in math class, prompted by assessment items in texts, prepared worksheets, and state tests. Unfortunately, when an explanation is not related to a meaningful task or when four to six problems are given to solve and explain but are never discussed, students often view this writing as something they do for others, rather than for themselves. We can counteract this perspective when we do the following:

- take time for students to share responses so that they can celebrate what they know, experience an authentic audience other than the teacher, and learn from others;
- provide tasks that interest students and warrant explanations;
- offer tasks that can be solved in a variety of ways to heighten interest in seeing, hearing, and reading the different ways students find solutions; and
- honor students' personal voices in their explanations.

Years ago, math problems often ended with *Show your work*. Today, it is more common to see *Explain your thinking*. Responses to this prompt might include the following:

- representations,
- calculations,
- calculation strategies,
- identification of problem-solving strategies,
- labels and words that connect calculations to the problem context,
- number sentences, and
- a clearly identified answer/solution.

Though some explanations include justifications, they do not have to—students are communicating what they did, not defending it.

Melissa Webster's second-grade students had been learning about addition and money. She had created some advertisements with pictures of products and whole-number prices. Students had "shopped" for two or three items and written "sales slips." To build on this idea, Melissa gave them this multistep problem about shopping:

Lucy buys two books and a video game on sale.
Each book costs the same amount.
The video game costs $39.00.
She spends $57.00 in all.
How much does each book cost?

Melissa believed that students' familiarity with the setting would support their productive struggle with the problem as well as give them something to write about. It did.

In pairs, the students took turns reading the problem together, one line at a time. After each line was read, the other student repeated it in his or her own words. Then Melissa asked Nadine to dramatize the problem. Nadine picked up the two books and video game that were on the table, and Melissa asked the class, "What is happening in the story?" Everyone agreed that Nadine was buying the books and the game. Melissa asked, "What does she have to do now?" After students said Nadine needed to pay, Melissa asked, "And how much do these items cost in all?" There was a chorus of "Fifty-seven dollars." Then Melissa said, "I want you to go back to your seats and work on this problem. Think about what else you know and what you have to find out."

As the students wrote, Melissa noticed that their explanations varied widely. When they finished, she asked them to explore their recorded ideas in groups of three. She told them, "First you sit and look at everyone's work. When I tell you it's time, one person will talk about what he or she wrote, while others listen. Next, the listeners will tell how their work is the same or different. Then it will be another person's turn to explain." Melissa showed the students this list to help them remember the directions:

1. Look at all the work.
2. Listen to one person.
3. Tell how your work is the same or different.
4. Repeat from Step 2.

Figure 5.2
Casey's
explanation

Casey, Gabriella, and Ruby formed a group. When Melissa announced it was time for listening to one person, Casey picked up his paper. He had relied on words in his explanation (Figure 5.2), which focused on his use of a "friendly number" to find the difference between 39 and 57. He communicated his thinking by reading what he wrote: "I added 1 to the 39 to make 40 and 40 to 57 is

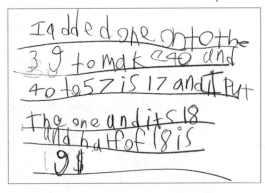

17, and I put the 1 and its 18, and half of 18 is $9.00." When Casey finished, Gabriella looked at her own response and said, "I found half of 18, too."

Gabriella's response (Figure 5.3) included multiple representations. She said, "I started with a picture and a number sentence to help me remember what the problem was about. I like using number lines. I found that 39 + 18 = 57." She pointed to the hops on her number line to illustrate how they helped her. After a pause, Casey said, "I like your number line. I could make one for how I added up to 57." Gabriella and Ruby agreed.

Figure 5.3
Gabriella's explanation

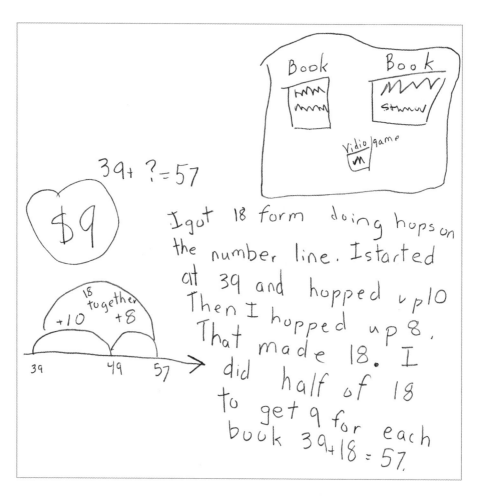

Ruby (Figure 5.4) reported, "I started with a picture of the video game and its cost. Then I counted to get to 57. Then I counted again to get 18. [She pointed at her numbers 0–18 as she said this.] I know 9 plus 9 is 18, so that was my answer."

Gabriella said, "Wait: I didn't get how you counted again on top."

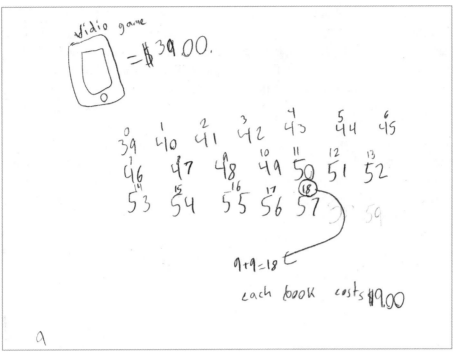

Figure 5.4
*Ruby's
explanation*

Ruby pointed to her paper and said, "I started at 39 and counted to 57. Then I had to count how many hops that was. There were 18 counts."

Gabriella seemed satisfied, but Casey still looked uncertain. After a pause, he asked, "Why did you start with zero?"

Ruby replied, "Thirty-nine wasn't a hop. I already spent that on the game. It was just where I started."

Because these students all knew the problem situation well and were given time to look closely at written responses, they were able to make important connections between the problem and their different representations and strategies. They also got a glimpse of what was unclear and might require a fuller written explanation. What an important conversation for these young learners to have about why Ruby started her count at zero.

How to Use a Procedure

Explaining how to do something gives students the opportunity to discover that they may use procedures that are different from those of their peers, gain a better conceptual understanding of a particular procedure, and/or uncover an error or misconception. Take a quick look back at the fraction "wodb" story that began on page 50. That was the beginning of a lesson I taught to fourth graders in early December. They had studied equivalent fractions and begun to investigate comparison of fractions. I was concerned that the lessons in their text were moving students to exclusive use of an algorithmic approach without, perhaps, complete understanding or paying enough attention to using benchmark numbers such as zero, one-half, and one. Often, comparison to a benchmark number is all students need to order fractions, and such thinking builds number sense. I chose pictures for the wodb task that I hoped would prompt students to make comparisons based on visual information. They did, though comparative ideas came later in the conversation. I was curious to see if that thinking would carry over to their next task, which was to write about the question *How can you tell if a fraction is less than, greater than, or equal to one-half?*

Excited by their ability to generate several responses to the wodb task, students began writing immediately and explained a variety of techniques. A significant number of students started by writing about rules they could use. For example, Lacey wrote, *I can tell if a fraction is less than $\frac{1}{2}$ because the bigger the denominator, the smaller the pieces,* but she did not note that the numerators had to be the same.

Celina and Noah worked next to each other. Celina began by writing about fractions she knew were equal to one-half. Her opening sentence suggests she understood that the numerator should be half of the denominator. She then included several drawings to show equivalent relationships. Meanwhile, Noah was busy writing about what several students referred to as the "multiplication rule." He gave three examples of how multiplying by a fraction equivalent to one could be used to determine whether a number was equal to, greater than, or less than one-half. His examples were clear, though he may or may not have understood why the approach worked.

When they were finished, I encouraged them to talk to each other about what they had written. I overheard Noah say, "I like the way you think about one-half." They spoke briefly about how that thinking could be applied to numbers that were greater or less than one. Then Celina said, "I have some ideas to add." Noah said he did too, and both students added new sections to their writing. Celina's and Noah's responses are shown in Figure 5.5. Celina provided a clear summary at the bottom of her paper. Noah included three new sections. He first compared $\frac{1}{2}$ to $\frac{1}{4}$, then $\frac{25}{50}$ to $\frac{1}{2}$, and then $\frac{2}{6}$ to $\frac{1}{2}$. Noah also returned to his opening words and added a second sentence to introduce this new idea. (Note that his second sentence is written in smaller letters, so he can fit it in.)

Even in this fairly objective type of writing, individual students' voices are present. In the section where Noah compared $\frac{2}{6}$ and $\frac{1}{2}$, I was drawn to his statement that 2 is not *yet* half of 6. Celina's opening sentences are conversational, with the potential to capture a reader's interest. The label for her drawings and the underlining of her comment *work to make sure!* communicate her interest in clearly conveying her thinking and her enthusiastic attitude.

It was wonderful to see how Celina and Noah's conversation informed their thinking. Celina extended her initial idea to fractions less than and greater than one-half. Noah was open to another approach, one I suspect he understood more fully.

Allocating time in the middle of a series of lessons or unit for students to write about a procedure, strategy, or concept gives them a powerful way to make their thinking explicit and for teachers to gain important formative assessment data. It allows different students to share different approaches and perhaps, as Noah did, adopt the thinking of their peers. There is an energy to writing at this formative stage that comes from students making meaning. Doing this writing can be a joyful experience for both students and teachers.

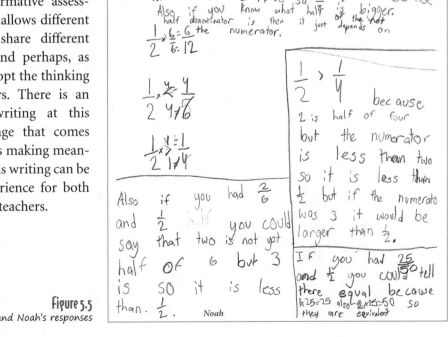

Figure 5.5
Celina's and Noah's responses

Explaining and Describing Mathematical Tools

The fourth standard for mathematical practice sets the expectation that students use tools appropriately (National Governors Association Center for Best Practices and Council of Chief State School Officers 2010a). At the elementary level, tools include manipulatives, measuring devices, calculators, and computers. Tools such as tally marks, tables, and graphs are used to keep track of and organize information.

Tally Marks

An explanatory task at the end of a lesson or unit can serve to clarify learning. After a week in which her students explored tally marks, first-grade teacher Christine Zybert closed math time by asking students to respond to the prompt *What can you tell me about a tally mark?* Note that the question suggests that Christine really wants to know what they think. Christine told me that the students were proud of what they knew and wrote about it with enthusiasm. Two responses are shown in Figure 5.6.

Both students communicated important ideas. Ali indicated the usefulness of tally marks, whereas Parisa gave more attention to the mechanics of how to use them. I wonder how Ali would respond to the question *How do they help us count?* or what Parisa would say if asked, *Why do a lot of people use tally marks?* It can be challenging, sometimes, to know when to follow up with students and when to accept their responses and move on. Time is always a factor. Christine chose to place this work in the students' portfolios, which allowed her to accept their current thinking while allowing for follow-up at a later date.

Figure 5.6
Ali's and Parisa's responses

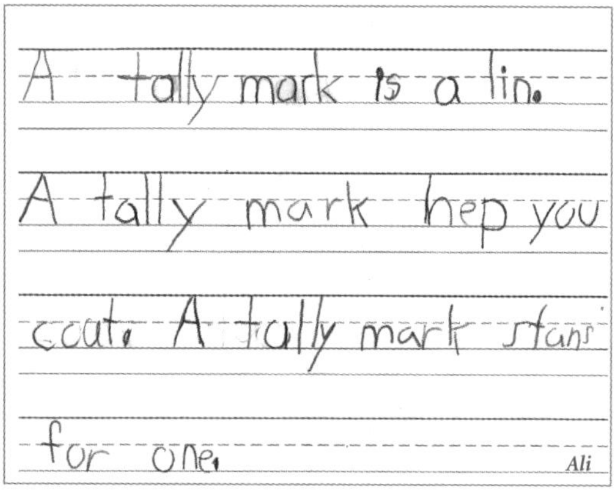

A tally mark is a lin. A tally mark hep you ccat. A tally mark stans for one.

Ali

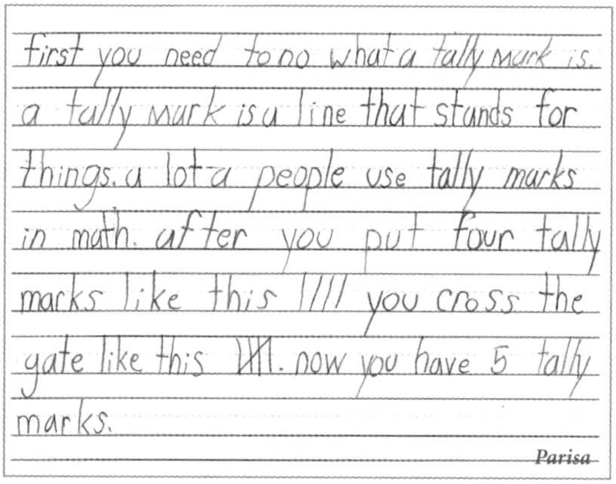

first you need to no what a tally mark is. a tally mark is a line that stands for things. a lot a people use tally marks in math. after you put four tally marks like this |||| you cross the gate like this ||||. now you have 5 tally marks.

Parisa

Rulers

When asked to write what they would tell a younger friend about a ruler, second-grade students emphasized different aspects of the tool. Kathy O'Connell Hopping introduced the lesson by asking students to think independently for thirty seconds and then tell one thing they knew about rulers as she jotted their ideas on the whiteboard. Inches, half inches, and centimeters were mentioned first, which led to the ideas that a centimeter was about the width of their finger and shorter than an inch. When Rodney mentioned that you could measure short and long lengths, Uma said, "We need to put *yardstick* in our list." After a few more ideas were shared, Kathy introduced the writing assignment.

The students wrote independently and provided a variety of information about rulers. As they wrote, Kathy thought about which responses she wanted them to share with the class. She was familiar with *5 Practices for Orchestrating Productive Mathematical Discussions* (Smith and Stein 2011) and knew the importance of selecting work that supported the points she wanted to make and ordering them in a way that would maximize learning.

She decided to begin by having Travis (Figure 5.7) project his response on the whiteboard. As many students did, Travis wrote about the equivalency between twelve inches and one foot. Kathy was pleased that he also indicated that an inch was about the size of an eraser. The students had recently investigated how knowing the measures of common objects could help them estimate lengths, and she wanted others to see it in Travis's response.

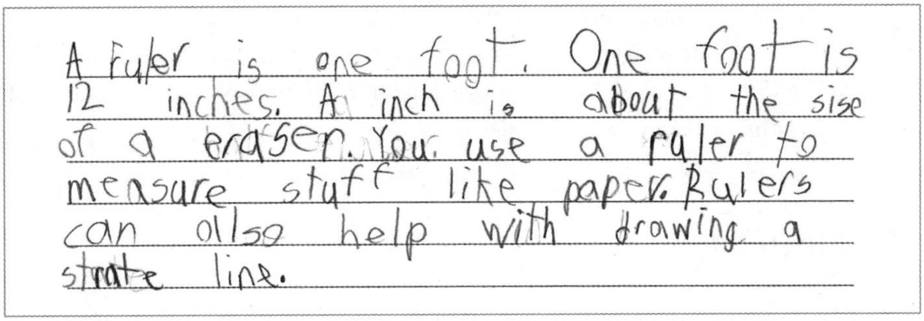
A ruler is one foot. One foot is 12 inches. A inch is about the sise of a eraser. You use a ruler to measure stuff like paper. Rulers can allso help with drawing a strate line.

Figure 5.7 Travis's response

She decided that Ivy (Figure 5.8) would present next. Ivy included a representation of the approximate length of both an inch and a centimeter. She then wrote about how to use a ruler to measure, giving two examples. Kathy knew students would easily follow this explanation but wanted them to hear it, because so many of them had not written anything similar.

She wanted Reese (Figure 5.9) to share his work last, because it introduced two new ideas. Though current standards do not require second graders to

Figure 5.8
Ivy's
response

A ruler has 12 inches. An inch is about this long.
| | 12 inches equals one foot. There are 30 centimeters in a ruler.
A centimeter is about this long. | | You can use a ruler to
make a straight line. There are numbers on a ruler.
If something is up to the number 5, that means it is
5 inches long. If something is to the number 7, it is 7 inches
long, and so on. That is how you measure with a ruler.

Figure 5.9
Reese's
response

You can use a ruler for many different things. But you cant
use a ruler for measuring liquid, or the amounts and weight
of things. There are inches, and centemctors on a ruler; There
are deviding lines to split things into halves, quarters, or
even smaller! A ruler is one foot long, or 30 centemeters
long. There are also half ruler/six inche rulers wich are the
same as regular rulers except its split in-half.

measure or estimate to the quarter inch, Reese wrote about the lines on a ruler that indicate parts of an inch. His phrase *or even smaller!* suggests he finds this subdivision of units interesting. He also wrote that rulers could not be used for measuring liquids or weight. Kathy wanted to expose students to these different ideas and thought they would be more receptive after listening to ideas that were more familiar.

Math in Nature

When I ask elementary students how they use math in their lives, they usually mention ideas such as keeping score, counting money, and telling time. I want them to realize that math can be seen all around them, and can inform their thinking about the world. The following example shows one way these more general goals can be supported.

Kathy O'Connell Hopping took a group of third graders on a mathematical nature walk. Armed with tablets, they walked out to a wetlands trail and board-walk behind their school. Their task was to look at their surroundings through the lens of a mathematician. In groups of two or three, they were to find their

Figure 5.10
Students working in a group and taking a picture

Figure 5.11
Eduardo and Kade's photo

own spot, take a picture, and then describe, in writing, what their mathematical eyes saw. (See Figure 5.10.)

Eduardo and Kade took a picture of the boardwalk (see Figure 5.11). They created their description as a write-around, each adding a sentence as they passed the response sheet between them. (Their written response is shown in Figure 5.12.) Their "zero" is actually the cross section of a log, and can be seen faintly in the upper right portion of their picture, above the boardwalk.

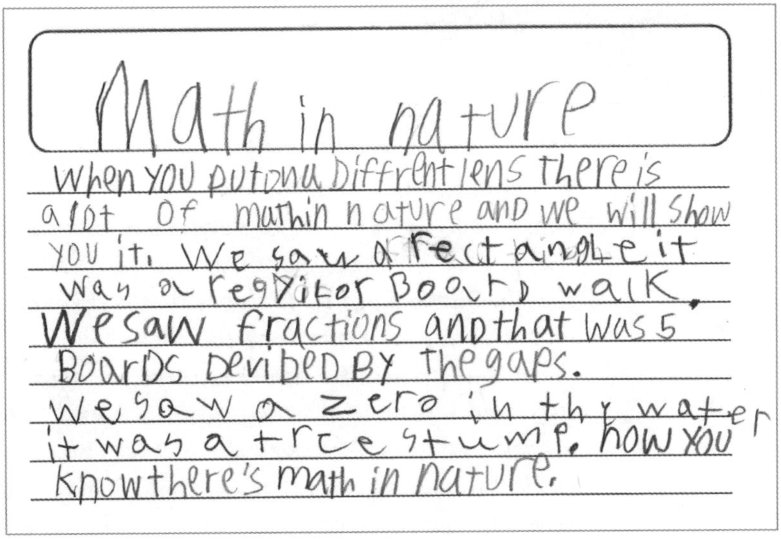

Figure 5.12
Eduardo and Kade's description

> ## Math in nature
>
> When you put on a diffrent lens there is a lot of math in nature and we will show you it. We saw a rectangle it way a regbitor Boolrd walk. We saw fractions and that was 5 Boards devibed By the gaps. We saw a zero in the water it was a tree stump. how you know there's math in nature.

Aki and Cory decided to measure the depth of the water near the board-walk (see Figure 5.13), which was a way to use math to learn more about what they saw. Together, they decided what to write, with Aki recording their thinking (Figure 5.14). After describing the many angles that they saw, they wrote *isn't that cool*, expressing their excitement about their discoveries.

Figure 5.13
Aki and Cory's photo

Nature Math

We went on a walk and looked at a boardwalk but wait wee see math we sre... Watter and we were seriouse how deep the watter was. So we ran inside and got a yard stick and we meashured the watter and we found 15 inchs! So we meashured all around but it was not the same length. We also saw angles behind the yard stick was a group of sticks, and branches and if you conect them it forms abtuce angles, and acute angles, and right angles is'nt that cool. We also saw numbers and letters from the reaflections of the sticks and branches. we saw a Y, Y, H, x, T and other letters and numbers. We also saw shapes in the watter like a circle a triangle and a. rectangle. Are there adicinall eyes staring at us from below. Theys are all the cool mathimatical things we saw with our math brains on the board walk.

Figure 5.14
Aki and Cory's description

Kathy's Reflection

I had never done this activity before and wasn't sure how the students would react. I knew they were familiar with the boardwalk. Starting in kindergarten our students do nature walks there, and a few teachers take classes there to write poems or sketch. But looking at the boardwalk through a mathematical lens would be a new experience for them.

It was great! The students were engaged and seemed truly surprised by the math they saw. Jack and Izzie's picture focused on a stick that was bent over the water. They described it as a "half circle." I laughed when I read, <u>being mathematicians we saw it as a jump on the number line.</u> I never would have made that connection.

The students enjoyed seeing everyone's picture and hearing what they wrote. They rarely share their math writing with the whole class, but the interest level was high, and it gave them all the chance to make their work public. The best part was the next day when I saw Olive. With excitement in her voice she said, "Ms. O'Connell, I'm seeing math everywhere!"

Math and Nonfiction Texts

I recently discovered *Animals by the Numbers: A Book of Infographics* by Steve Jenkins. As the author writes, "In this book, facts and figures about animals are presented visually as graphics, symbols, and illustrations" (2016, 3). I loved that it provided so much numerical data about animals in such an accessible manner. I showed the book to Title 1 specialist Jennifer Spencer and third-grade teacher Lina Lopez-Ryan. Jen and Lina coteach math, and I suggested that they might want to share this book with their students. In response, they added mathematics to an interdisciplinary unit of study that Lina knew she would be teaching later that spring. The experience was so rich that I have included several examples of math-related writing that resulted.

It began with Lucy Calkins and Kathleen Toban's (2015) "Research Clubs: Elephants, Penguins, and Frogs, Oh My!," a research-based unit on the study of animals. Lina organized crates of books, sorted by animal, and formed "clubs" of three to four students who would conduct research on one animal (see Figure 5.15). Two weeks later, they considered a second animal and then compared and contrasted the two. After about a month, students were quite familiar with their animals and their books.

Figure 5.15
Reference books

Math was introduced into the unit when Jen shared a few selected pages from *Animals by the Numbers*. The students marveled at the "giants" when she showed them the page that compared sizes of large animals with humans. They were intrigued by the number of years some animals have been extinct, and even wondered if there were a connection between animal size and years of extinction. When they saw the visual representation of the number of hours different animals sleep, students spontaneously compared their own sleeping habits with those of giraffes, cats, and squirrels. Steven commented, "I never knew there were so many numbers about animals." To further tap students' curiosity, Lina and Jen asked them to think about what numerical information they might want to know about the animals they were studying. The students enthusiastically explored their ideas by recording questions in their journals. Amanda's questions are shown in Figure 5.16.

Figure 5.16
Amanda's list of questions

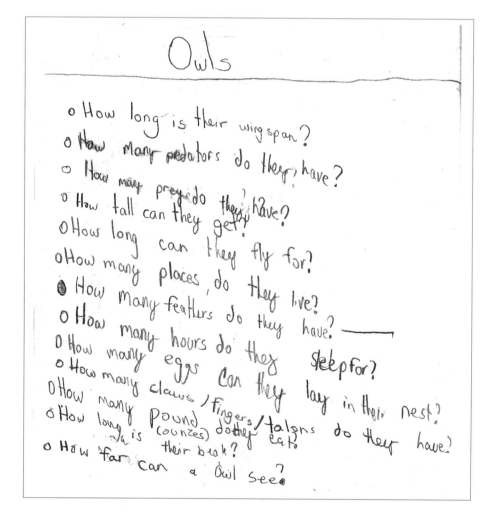

Then, Lina and Jen asked students to look at one of their nonfiction books through a mathematical lens. The students were amazed by how much math they found. "Math is everywhere" was heard throughout the room. Naomi asked, "Are there math words in fiction, too?" Jenna's journal entry (Figure 5.17) captured thoughts shared by many of the students.

Figure 5.17
Jenna's journal entry expressing her reaction

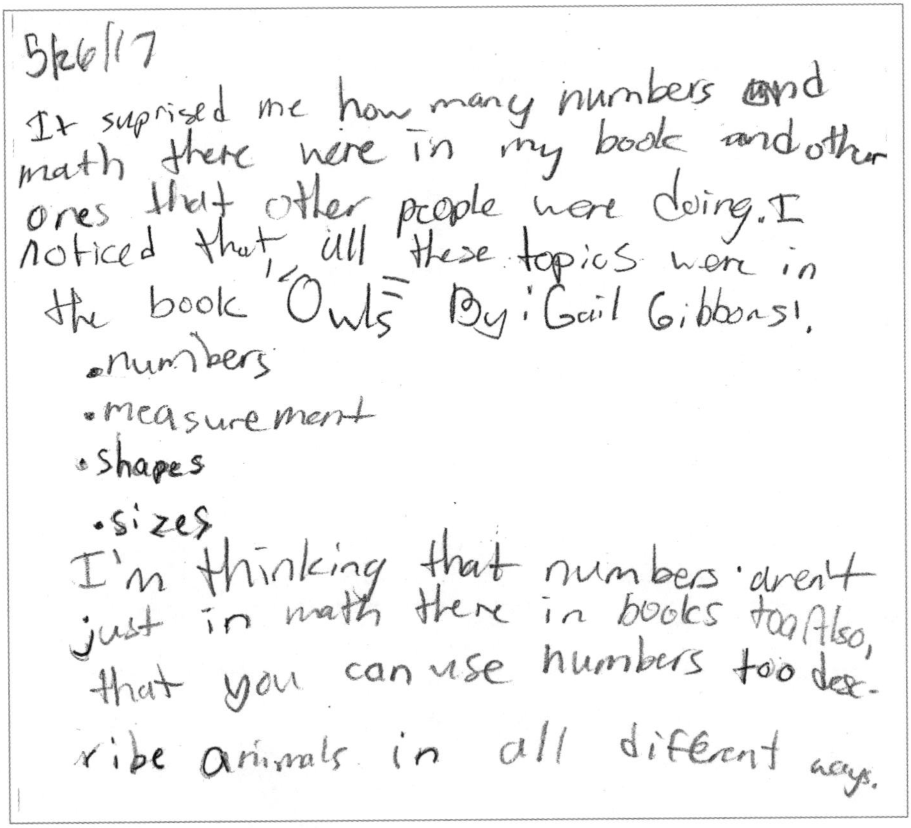

5/26/17

It suprised me how many numbers and math there were in my book and other ones that other people were doing. I noticed that, all these topics were in the book "Owls" By: Gail Gibbons!.

• numbers
• measurement
• shapes
• sizes

I'm thinking that numbers aren't just in math there in books too Also, that you can use numbers too describe animals in all diffrent ways.

Lina and Jen were not surprised by the students' reactions. In their planning, they each randomly chose a book from the crates and experimented with this task. As they read silently, they kept interrupting each other to read a math-related sentence they had found. They said it seemed as if they had put math glasses on and phrases such as *below freezing temperatures* and *about 100 times* were suddenly written in bold. They immediately recognized that these salient examples offered a springboard for inquiry-based math learning and discussion.

Next, the students listed some of the "number facts" they found about their animals and made a personal connection to each piece of information. While doing so, students often stopped and made physical models to better understand the data they gathered. Gemma told Lina that twenty feet was about the length of her puppy. When Lina asked how we could find out how long twenty feet was, yardsticks and rulers were lined across the floor. Gemma discovered that twenty feet was much longer than she originally thought. The charts that Jules and Autumn completed are shown in Figure 5.18. Notice how the connec-

Figure 5.18
Facts and
connections

THE MATH	THE CONNECTION
Number Fact	This makes me *wonder* . . . This reminds me of... This surprises me because...
Raccoons can weigh 35 pounds	This makes me wonder if one of my cats, Mocha, weighs somewhere around a raccoon.
Raccoons can measure 28" long	That's almost as long as 2 rulers.
A raccoon's territory usually stays smaller than 2 square-miles	This makes me think of the mile run.
Newborn kits weigh just over 2 ounces	I wonder what else weighs 2 ounces.
At 5 months of age, raccoons go out with their mothers at night.	That means that they are almost half a year-old.
Kits do not open their eyes until they're 20 days old	This makes me wonder how long it takes for a human to open their eyes.

Jules

THE MATH	THE CONNECTION
Number Fact	This makes me *wonder* . . . This reminds me of... This surprises me because...
Beavers weigh around 45-60 pounds.	heavy!! a kit only weighs 1 pound!
A beaver can cut trough a 6-inch-thick tree with its sharp orange teeth in less than 20 minutes.	I couldn't even saw trough 6 inches!
Beavers can live to be 20.	That is young! Humans can live up to 80!
With their strong paddle-shaped tails and webbed feet, beavers can swim at a speed of up to 2 miles per hour.	That is slow compared to a car.
A beavers sharp sence of smell is about 100 times better than ours.	I want to small that well.
Beavers usually can stay underwater for 3 to 5 minutes.	I cant even stay underwater for 1 minute.

Autumn

tion column helps students make sense of the descriptive facts. The students gave particular attention to measures. To make them more meaningful, students converted them to other units or compared them with something they knew. Also, note that given the chance to wonder, they were still identifying new questions to pursue.

The next day, students made tables to summarize the numerical data they were discovering. They learned about using *N/A* and discovered that organizing their information this way helped them notice comparisons. Louie's table is shown in Figure 5.19. He was quite surprised by how much longer most owls live in captivity. He remarked, "This really makes me understand what predators are all about." What a great example of how quantitative data can inform our understanding of a situation!

Animal: __Owls__   There are __140__ species of this animal.

N/A = not applicable

Species	Height	Length	Weight	Life Span in Captivity	Life Span in the Wild	OTHER Number facts
elf owl	5½ in	N/A	1.4 ounces	3 to 6 years	3 to 6 years	
saw whet owl	7 in	N/A	males is 75 grams female is 100 grams	16 years	7 years	
burrowing owl	9 in	N/A	6 ounces	10 years	6 to 8 years	
great horned owl	18 to 25 in	N/A	6 pounds	50 years	28 years	
great grey owl	24 to 33 in	N/A	2 to 4 pounds	27 years	16 years	

Figure 5.19
Louie's table

The final math-related task of the unit was for students to describe their animals, using and underlining a math word in each sentence. Dalila's response is shown in Figure 5.20. Note that she included numbers as well as terms and tools used in math such as *longest, each,* and *ruler.*

Amari provided an overview (Figure 5.21) and then focused on two stages in the life of a beaver. Lina noted that Amari had incorporated both comparative and sequential information, two text structures they had studied during the unit.

This is an interdisciplinary unit that many students will remember for years. I suspect that most of those who studied beavers, owls, or raccoons will

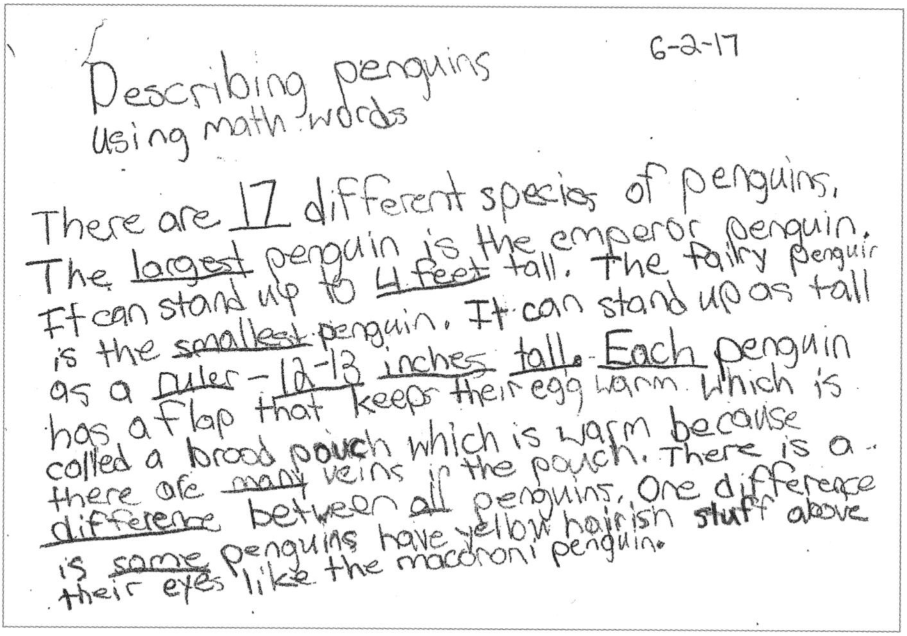

Figure 5.20
Dalila's
description

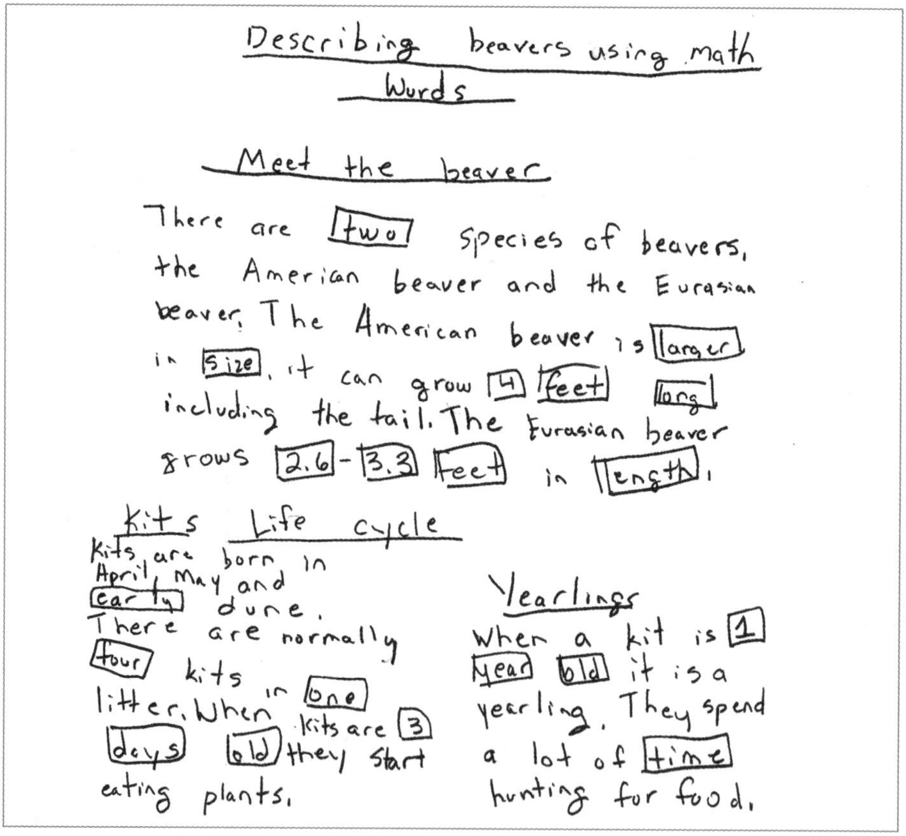

Describing penguins
using math words

6-2-17

There are 17 different species of penguins.
The largest penguin is the emperor penguin.
It can stand up to 4 feet tall. The Fairy penguin
is the smallest penguin. It can stand up as tall
as a ruler — 12-13 inches tall. Each penguin
has a flap that keeps their egg warm. Which is
called a brood pouch which is warm because
there are many veins in the pouch. There is a
difference between all penguins. One difference
is some penguins have yellow hairish stuff above
their eyes like the macaroni penguin.

Figure 5.21
Amari's
description

Describing beavers using math
Words

Meet the beaver

There are two species of beavers,
the American beaver and the Eurasian
beaver. The American beaver is larger
in size, it can grow 4 feet long
including the tail. The Eurasian beaver
grows 2.6 - 3.3 feet in length.

Kits Life cycle
Kits are born in
April, May and
early June.
There are normally
four kits in
litter. When kits are 3
days old they start
eating plants.

Yearlings
When a kit is 1
year old it is a
yearling. They spend
a lot of time
hunting for food.

have a sense of familiarity whenever they see one. This particular topic or length of unit may or may not be right for your students, but I encourage you to do the following:

- have students notice the math in nonfiction texts,
- provide opportunities for students to organize numerical data in ways that make comparisons more obvious,
- encourage students to make personal connections to data they read, and
- apply a mathematical lens to other units of study.

Embracing Opportunities

You can plan opportunities for students to explain and describe their thinking, but sometimes it just comes up naturally. A "Number of Days in School" chart in Becky Eston Salemi's kindergarten classroom is marked each day in morning meeting. Becky knows her students are required to count only to one hundred, but appreciates how students use the chart throughout the year to anchor their growing understanding of our number system. She is always fascinated when the chart sparks new ideas. Near the end of the school year, when the chart was almost complete, several children began to ask questions about what happened after 180. For some this was a query about ending kindergarten. Others wanted to know, "What about 200?" "What about 1,000?"

Zac was leaving the rug area when he stopped to look at the chart. He pondered it for a moment, and then began a conversation with Becky.

> *Zac*: There's a pattern to the zeros.
> *Becky*: Tell me more about that.
> *Zac*: It goes zero, one, two. You get more each time.
> *Becky*: That sounds interesting. What do you mean by *more each time?*
> *Zac*: Can I write it down?
> *Becky*: Of course. That's a great way to tell me, and others, more about your thinking.
> *Zac*: It's cool. Wait until you see.

Becky wasn't sure what Zac meant about the zeros, but she could tell it was important to him, and she genuinely wanted to understand more about his idea. Determined to explain his discovery to his teacher, Zac went to where writing supplies were kept in the room and chose a piece of paper that had both lined and unlined spaces for recording. He began writing as soon as he sat

Figure 5.22
Zac's explanation of the number of zeros

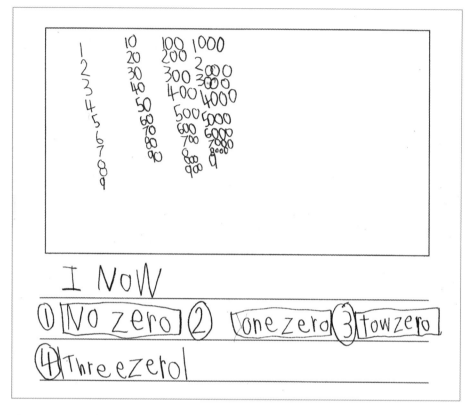

down. His work is shown in Figure 5.22. Note his meticulous use of columns in the blank space as though they were an illustration. Including the numbered labels in the lined section shows that he understood that his piece needed more information.

Many aspects of this story seem significant to me. It's a great reminder of the curiosity students bring to the classroom, along with a desire to make sense of the world. Zac was eager to describe the pattern he noticed, and recognized that the easiest way to do so would be in writing. The numbers he chose to record indicate that he intuitively recognized the importance of place value and multiples of ten. His work reminds me not to underestimate the thinking of young learners. And, it illustrates many of the aspects of Becky's classroom that I have always loved. Over the course of the year, her young students become empowered to support their own learning. They are given opportunities to choose the materials they will use, the ways they will communicate their thinking, and the ideas they will pursue. It is in such a learning environment that her students become mathematicians, explaining their own thinking about mathematical ideas they consider interesting. And recording their ideas helps them flourish.

Closing Thoughts

When we create communities where new thinking is welcomed, our students' thoughts can amaze us. When students pursue engaging tasks, their responses are usually quite interesting, too. Consequently, we are eager to read such writing, to learn what students have noticed and wondered. This anticipation and excitement is quite different from what we feel when we look at a pile of work that needs to be "corrected."

6 Writing to Justify and Convince

Understanding why, along with what and how, helps students form important links between their procedural and conceptual knowledge. When students make a generalization such as *When you add two even numbers, you get an even sum* and then justify that claim with words and/or representations, they are creating a mathematical argument (Russell et al. 2017). Learners form an argument by asking questions, making judgments, creating generalizations or claims, defending decisions, selecting reasons, critiquing ideas, and drawing conclusions. Within this interactive process, writing becomes a way to both clarify and communicate thinking, and students can envision themselves as curious, appropriately skeptical mathematicians on a mission to discover mathematical meaning.

Emphasizing What and Why

To engage a class of third-grade students in thinking about *why*, I created a couple of "fit the facts" problems, which are short stories with blanks instead of numbers (Greenes, Schulman, and Spungin 1993, 284). Similar to what Brian Bushart (@Stocktus), coordinator for elementary math at the Round Rock

Independent School District in Texas, calls numberless problems, these problems begin without numbers. To learn more about Brian's thoughts on numberless problems, read his blog entry at https://bstockus.wordpress.com/2014/10/06/numberless-word-problems. I like to have students discuss what the missing numbers could be, and then I show them the "facts" and have students figure out where the data fit. This format gives students multiple entry points and supports development of their reasoning skills. They can also foster number, operation, and measurement sense.

When the third graders gathered in the rug area, I showed them the following information that was posted on easel paper and asked what they noticed. This problem format was new to them. Manny's first comment was "Wait, I thought we were doing math."

Colleen responded, "I think it's math, but there are no numbers."

Pablo said, "It looks like a story."

Marta is _____ years old and is in grade _____. Marta walks her dog every morning before going to school. She starts her walk at _____ o'clock and walks for _____ minutes. That's _____ minutes each week! Her _____ older sister walks the dog on weekends.

I invited students to think about what they knew about the missing numbers and how some of the numbers might be related. They considered the first sentence as a whole group. After some wait time, Rhianna suggested, "The numbers won't be really large, because after a while you don't go to school anymore."

Sophia said, "You're only in school from kindergarten to maybe college."

Matt added, "We need numbers, so I think it has to be one through twelve."

Laney said, "I agree with Matt. We need numbers."

I checked with the class, and with students' agreement, wrote *1–12* in the second blank because I wanted to model how they might record their initial ideas. Emmy then said, "I want to think about the ages of kids in those grades. I mean, it can't be just any age."

I asked, "How could we show that connection so we remember it?" Leo suggested drawing a line between the two blanks, and then Rita said we should make an arrow.

Joey said, "My brother is in first grade and he is six."

"I think you go to school until you're about sixteen," offered Liam.

The students decided that six through sixteen was about right. I wondered if I should tell them that most people are older than sixteen when they finish high school, but decided not to interrupt their thinking and ownership of this work. I recorded *6–16* in the first blank and asked the students to turn and talk to a partner about what they knew about the other numbers, reminding them to think about what made sense and how the numbers might be related. Their conversations lasted several minutes. When they began to quiet down, I brought their attention back and they discussed the remaining blanks.

The students recognized that the number of minutes each day was related to the number of minutes for each week. One-half of an hour was suggested for the duration of the daily walk, and others agreed until Chelsea pointed out that it was the number of minutes, not hours, so it could not be one-half. They decided thirty minutes was reasonable, and that the total number of minutes would be a big number. They had a longer discussion about the number of sisters. Several of the students thought it would likely be one to three but were later convinced by Elena, who said, "Wait. It's *sister*, not *sisters*. It has to be one."

Once all the blanks were considered, I asked the students if they would like to see the missing numbers. "Yes!" they chorused loudly, and Caleb exclaimed, "I'm so excited to see what they are!" After I revealed the missing numbers in a list below the text, I explained that I had not written them in order. Figure 6.1 shows what I recorded during the discussions, along with the missing numbers I provided. The students' next task was to talk in pairs about where the numbers belonged.

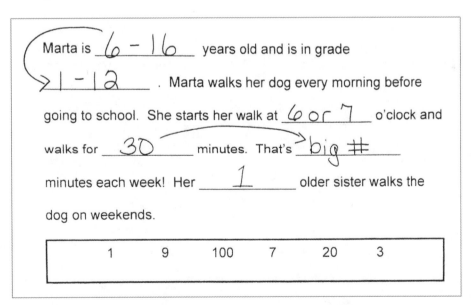

Figure 6.1
Problem with recordings and the missing numbers that were listed later

Animated conversations began immediately. When it was time to discuss their thinking as a whole group, I explained that I wanted to hear *what* they thought and *why* they thought so. My recording of their statements is shown in Figure 6.2.

Figure 6.2

Steps to solve: _what_ and _why_

Marta is ___6 – 16___ years old and is in grade

___1 – 12___ . Marta walks her dog every morning before

going to school. She starts her walk at ___6 or 7___ o'clock and

walks for ___30___ minutes. That's ___big #___

minutes each week! Her ___1___ older sister walks the

dog on weekends.

| 1 | 9 | 100 | 7 | 20 | 3 |

① 100 minutes is a big number.

② 20 minutes each day, 5 × 20 = 100
   20 + 20 + 20 + 20 + 20 = 100, used
   fingers to keep track.

③ 1 sister, it's not sisters.

④ grade 3 and 9 years fit together

⑤ 7 right time for getting to
   school and not walking in middle
   of night.

I then gave students a similar problem to consider at their tables, working independently or with a partner. I told them they would first think about what they knew about the numbers and that once they had recorded those ideas, I would give them a list of the number choices. When I gave them the numbers, I reminded them that their steps should involve what and why. The task, along with the number choices that were later revealed, is shown in Figure 6.3.

Hannah's response (Figure 6.4) shows that she recorded her initial ideas in the blanks and elaborated on them in the What We Know column. When she finished this list, she sat back and declared, "Wow, I know a lot!" When I identified the choices for the missing numbers, Hannah was excited to see the 3. She told me, "When I write what I know first, everything is easy."

I have always loved the puzzle-like format of these problems. It's a great vehicle for engaging students in making connections between _what_ and _why_, which is an important step in making sense of mathematical ideas. It was exciting to see how eager the students were to

Figure 6.3

The next problem the students investigated, along with the numbers revealed

| 120 | 3 | 7 | 14 | 2 | 21 | 24 |

Jake made a kite for each of his _____ younger brothers. They are triplets

and their birthday is November _____. The length of each kite is _____

feet or _____ inches. He painted _____ stripes on each of the kites for a

total of _____ stripes. He tied _____ feet of string to each kite.

total of _____ stripes. He tied _____ feet of string to each kite.

What We Know	Steps to Solve

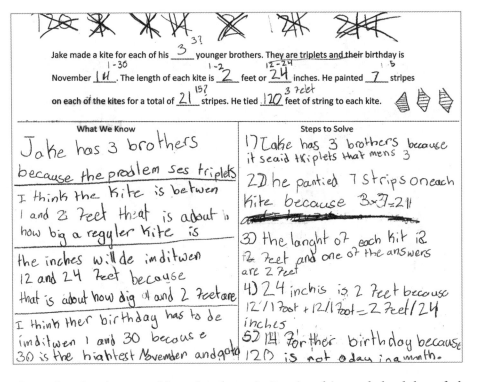

Figure 6.4
Hannah's
response

share what they knew and how they knew it. Starting this way helped them feel competent, and when I gave them the number choices, they moved seamlessly to that part of the task, immediately making connections to what they had already discovered. I noted that many of them kept track of the numbers they placed by crossing them out.

I wasn't sure how well they would do on their own, so I offered them the choice of sharing ideas with their tablemates. When I checked in at one table, three of the students were ready for the number choices, but one boy was still working on listing what he knew. He said, "You can show them the numbers, but I want to think more." I loved his perseverance, his willingness to hold off on getting more information until he was ready, and his thoughtfulness toward those who were ready to move forward with their work.

Curiosity and Skepticism

Interest in justifying ideas requires a combination of curiosity and skepticism. As you may have concluded from reading about the interdisciplinary animal unit in Chapter 5, curiosity is the norm in Lina Lopez-Ryan and Jennifer Spencer's math class. When their third graders are involved in an investigation,

Figure 6.5
Posting of
math
questions

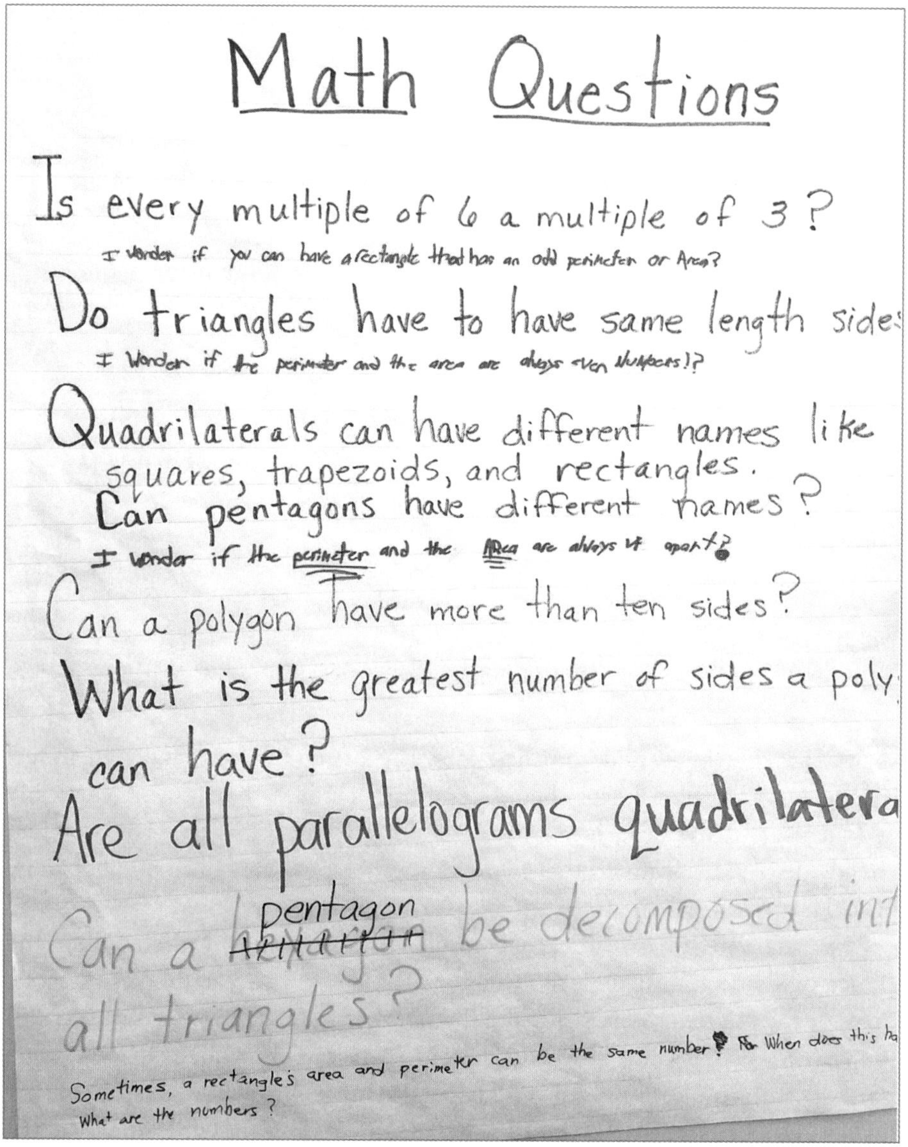

Math Questions

Is every multiple of 6 a multiple of 3?

I wonder if you can have a rectangle that has an odd perimeter or Area?

Do triangles have to have same length sides

I Wonder if the perimeter and the area are always even numbers)?

Quadrilaterals can have different names like squares, trapezoids, and rectangles.
Can pentagons have different names?

I wonder if the perimeter and the Area are always 4 apart?

Can a polygon have more than ten sides?

What is the greatest number of sides a poly can have?

Are all parallelograms quadrilatera

Can a ~~hexagon~~ pentagon be decomposed int all triangles?

Sometimes, a rectangle's area and perimeter can be the same number? & When does this ha

Sometimes, a rectangle's area and perimeter can be the same number? What are the numbers?

they are expected to be on the lookout for interesting, related questions. Those that arise are recorded, so that they can be returned to, and Lina and Jen build in class time for students to later explore those queries. Figure 6.5 shows their current list of math questions. The first one is from a lesson on multiplication. The others were posed during the three weeks the students were exploring shapes, area, and perimeter. Lina or Jen often record the questions at the end of a lesson. One of them might say, "Here are the questions I heard as we were working" or ask, "What math questions came up for you today?" Students record other questions as they arise. (Note the questions written in smaller text.) The publication of these questions, together with time to investigate them, honors students' curiosity and gives them new opportunities to justify ideas and convince others they are correct.

Can This Be True?

As teachers, we should also be on the lookout for interesting questions. Recently, Marty Daignault was on a weekend bicycle trip with his son, Lucas. They were riding through rural Vermont when they passed the cemetery where Calvin Coolidge is buried. As they rode in, Marty became curious about another gravestone that caught his eye. They stopped and read that Esther Sumner Damon was born in 1814, died in 1906, and was a widow of a soldier in the Revolutionary War. Marty's first reaction was one of skepticism. He thought, *Can this be true?* He had Lucas take a picture of the stone (Figure 6.6) and wondered what his fourth-grade students would make of this information.

That Monday morning, Marty told his students about biking in Vermont over the weekend, showed them the picture, and asked what they noticed. They read the dates, but with some quick math decided it was not possible, that a mistake had been made, or someone had lied or "lost" the truth in old age—maybe even Esther! Marty directed them to use the Internet to find more information about the Revolutionary War, soldiers' enlistment policy, and marriage laws. He encouraged them not to simply do a search of Esther's name, but rather, to have the fun of finding, organizing, and interpreting data from a variety of sources.

Students worked enthusiastically in groups of three or four, eager to learn more about this mystery. They took notes and discussed their conclusions. One group discovered that boys as young as six years old served in the war and decided this could have been true of Esther's husband. They used this fact to create a timeline they thought was feasible (Figure 6.7).

Figure 6.6
Lucas' picture of a gravestone from a Vermont cemetery

Figure 6.7
One group's
timeline of
events

Maybe he was born 1769
1775 start of revolutionary war
1781 they stopped fighting
1783 the war officialy ended

Groups of students shared their prized information and logic. Most groups thought it was possible that the tale was true but that it was highly unlikely. They thought it more probable that Esther was confused. One group found a website that said the greatest number of years any human had lived was 160, and incorporated it into their argument (Figure 6.8). Other students were skeptical that anyone had lived that long.

Figure 6.8
One group's
written
conclusion

The man who fought in the war was 76 years old when he got married. The girl was 21. The woman lived to 92 years old. The oldest person was 160 years old. It is possible.

When their work was completed, Marty shared the real data that he had found online: Esther was twenty-one years old when she married her husband, the veteran, who was seventy-five years old. All but one group accepted this finding. The last group accepted the math but still thought, "Someone so young would not marry someone so old!"

Students stayed engaged with this task for two math classes, using computation skills and number sense to interpret information related to history. It prompted a conversation about the need to verify data found online and demonstrated how useful timelines can be when one needs to organize information. It was also wonderful for them to see their teacher share both his

1814
Ester was
born

1835
they were
married

1906
Esther
Died

curiosity and his skepticism, to model that each day offers opportunities for noticing new, interesting information that can be validated with a mathematical argument. Although the information on the gravestone appeared to be true, it was important to tap into a healthy sense of skepticism.

It's Unreasonable

As part of their professional development, a group of teachers I worked with read Tracy Johnston Zager's wonderful book, *Becoming the Math Teacher You Wish You'd Had* (2017). Fifth-grade teacher Lisa Manzi was particularly interested in Tracy's story about Jennifer Clerkin Muhammad and the use of the sentence stem "I think _____ is unreasonable because _____" (p. 90). A few weeks after she read about this idea, her students measured their heights, in pairs, and recorded them on a poster chart. Her plans were for them to organize the data in a line plot. When Lisa looked at their measures, she was quite surprised to find 78 inches listed among them. The next day, she showed her class a typed list of heights recorded by fifth graders, but did not identify it as their own. She asked them to consider the data and complete the sentence frame if they thought any of the measures were unreasonable. Paco's response is shown in Figure 6.9. Note his phrase *rounds about 54" to 66"*. He is trying to communicate a range of heights that he would consider likely. Though not the mathematical definition of rounding, his statement makes sense.

I think _____ 78" _____ is unreasonable because _____ it would _____
be as tall as a very tall man it would be
over 6ft and a fifth grader usually rounds
about 54" to 66".

Figure 6.9
Paco's justification

Lisa's Reflection

I was so surprised when I saw 78 inches listed in their measures. The sticky notes had been posted so that everyone could see the data, and no one had challenged his or her own measure. I thought that looking at "anonymous" data would allow them to discover the error themselves, without embarrassing anyone. After our discussion, I asked them what they would say if their partners measured them and reported a height of 78 inches. They were clear that they would protest. I have incorporated this sentence frame several more times since this happened, and students have started to spontaneously use the phrase during our math talks. My students have become more aware of how important it is to be critical about mathematical results. I am so grateful for learning about this idea.

Using Familiar Contexts

Our younger students can also justify their thinking and critique the thinking of others. As with all students, asking them to do so within familiar contexts can support their success. Connecting to other subject areas and current events can capture students' interest in a math task as well as evoke a sense of confidence.

Ladybugs

Becky Eston Salemi's kindergartners had been observing the stages in the life cycle of ladybugs as part of their study of living things. Ladybugs had arrived in the mail in the larvae stage and less than two weeks later entered the pupa stage. During that stage, the ladybugs underwent metamorphosis, and finally they emerged as adult ladybugs. Once the transformation was complete, the ladybugs scurried around their enclosed environment.

When the students reviewed the stages of the growth cycle of the ladybugs, Becky asked them what they noticed about this current stage. Taylor exclaimed, "There are so many!" Everyone agreed; it appeared that the ladybugs' movement made it seem like there was a lot of them. Becky decided she wanted to follow up on Taylor's comment and said, "I wonder if you can count the ladybugs to find how many there are. What do you think?" When she asked the students whether they could count the ladybugs, thirteen raised their hands to say yes, and four raised their hands to say no.

Becky asked them to tell more about their thinking in writing. She encouraged them to write something that might persuade their classmates to change their minds. Malena and Alison both believed that the ladybugs could not be counted. Though different, their reasons (Figure 6.10) both related to the challenge of keeping track of the moving insects. Malena expressed her concern about counting the same one more than once. Alison was one of only a few students who explicitly indicated whether they agreed or disagreed. After reflecting further on the students' responses, Becky noted, "Both of their drawings of the ladybugs clearly indicate two antennae, six legs, and spots. I'm delighted to see that even when focused on a math task, students paid attention to facts they had learned about the anatomy of ladybugs."

Figure 6.10
Two responses from students who didn't believe they could be counted

Malena: Because I would count the same one.

Alison: I said no because the ladybugs were moving. So I couldn't count them.

Once the students discussed their reasoning with others, three of the original students who had said yes changed their thinking. Bain, however, continued to claim that it was possible to count the ladybugs they had been observing. His reason (Figure 6.11) was also related to keeping track of them; he claimed he could count them because they stopped moving. Though Becky was surprised that Bain stood by his conviction after many others were so persuasive

Figure 6.11
Bain's response

Because most of the ladybugs stopped.

about their reasoning, she also inwardly applauded him for not wavering in his stance. She thought back to an earlier time in the year when counting much smaller sets of stationary objects was challenging for many students in this class. Just like the ladybugs, her students had been transformed. Not only were they aware of one-to-one correspondence, but they could now reason mathematically, share their thinking with others, and write about their ideas in clear and concise ways. The students had taken what they knew about what makes it challenging to count large sets of objects and connected it to this query. Exciting!

Figure 6.12
Examples of lists

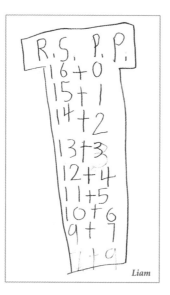

Sasha

Liam

Opening Day

Opening day of the baseball season in the Boston area is a big event. Christine Zybert's first-grade students have been investigating all the possible combinations of addends for a given sum. She decided to first have students explore sums to sixteen in connection with the baseball game, and then follow up with a task that would give them the opportunity to justify their thinking. On the morning of the big game, she read them the following task:

Ms. Z predicts that the combined runs of today's Red Sox game with the Pittsburgh Pirates will be 16. What are the possible combinations of runs for the two teams?

Students' ability to find all of the combinations varied. Liam's and Sasha's lists are shown in Figure 6.12. Liam labeled his addends and made a connection to his knowledge of baseball when he explained, "I didn't write 8 + 8 because someone has to win the game." Then he forgot about this context and focused on what he knew about addition. He erased 7 + 9 from his list and stopped there because, "The numbers just turn around here. They are the same numbers." Sasha found all of the combinations. She started with $10 + 6 = 16$ and $0 + 16 = 16$ and explained, "I like to start with the easy facts." From there, she listed the combinations in an organized manner, remembering to omit the facts she had already identified. Sasha then began to write number sentences with three addends, but erased them when she remembered that there were only two teams.

Having established the context of baseball scores, Christine posted the following task the next day. She told me she wanted to give students an opportunity to state a claim and defend it, and knew her students would enjoy her error.

> *Ms. Z predicted that the total number of runs scored would be 16.*
> *The score was Red Sox, 5 runs and Pirates, 3 runs.*
> *Was Ms. Z correct? How do you know?*

This was the students' first experience of challenging someone's thinking in writing. They were certain that their teacher was incorrect. Their confidence allowed them to fully focus on how they wanted to justify their decision. Lillian's responses is shown in Figure 6.13. Notice that she uses a graphic to display the information and clearly claims that Ms. Z. was wrong. She defends her claim by writing that $5 + 3 = 8$, not 16. Don't you love that she is sorry to have to communicate this negative feedback?

Figure 6.13
Sample
justification

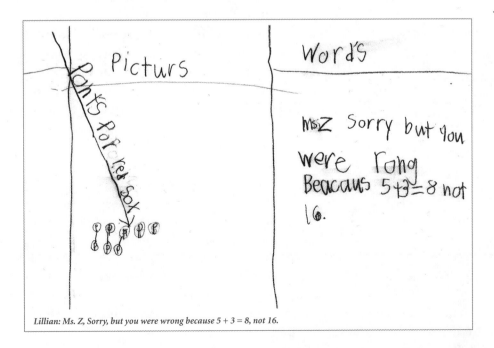

Lillian: Ms. Z, Sorry, but you were wrong because 5 + 3 = 8, not 16.

Building Theories with Representations

Whenever I think about the success of all learners, I remember the importance of visual models, both in the tasks we offer and in students' responses. Just as illustrations help readers understand the meaning of a story, visual representations help students comprehend math situations. Visual patterns can stimulate students to make generalizations. Teacher Fawn Nguyen (@fawnpnguyen) has created a magnificent resource of visual patterns appropriate for upper-elementary or middle school students to investigate that may also give you ideas for the younger grades. You can find them at http://www.visualpatterns.org/.

Kathy O'Connell Hopping offered fifth graders the task shown in Figure 6.14. The students were experienced at finding and expressing patterns in tables, but had not worked with visual models. After an opportunity for them to notice that the bridges were growing and for a few students to make predictions about the next few bridges, Kathy pointed out that the representation shown was two-dimensional and that if they wanted to make a drawing, they didn't have to draw three-dimensional blocks. She also reminded them that when they found an answer, they needed to convince others that it was correct. This challenge captured students' attention. Leo said, "I'm going to convince everyone that I am right."

As students explored the task, some made tables and some made drawings. Most found the answer of 152 within a few minutes, but as they changed their focus to convincing others of their conclusion, many students began to look more closely at the structure of the bridges and how they were growing. In this process, several students moved from the specific case (bridge 50) to a generalization that would always work. Such thinking brought them closer to what mathematicians consider proof. Several students began to use color to help them. Erica's work went through three stages. She first summarized information in a table (Figure 6.15) to help her create a general formula.

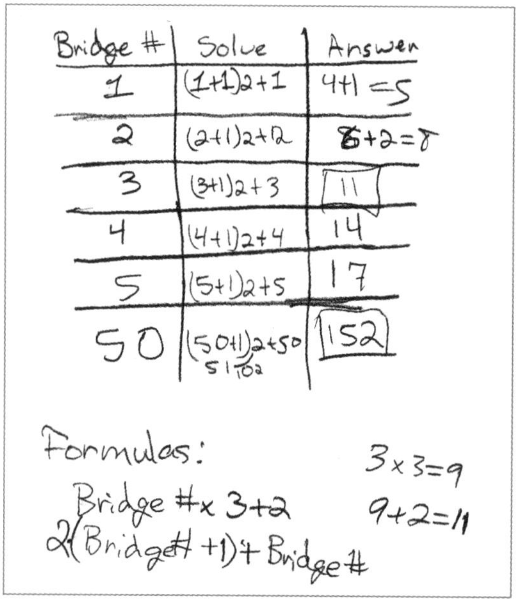

Figure 6.14
Growing bridges task

Jason's younger sister was building bridges with blocks.

bridge 1   bridge 2   bridge 3

How many blocks will be needed to build bridge 50?

How could you convince your classmates that you are correct?

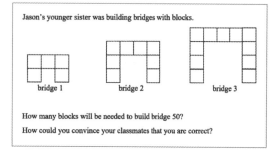

Figure 6.15
Erica's table

Having found a generalization, which she represented with two equations, she wanted to be sure her argument was clear and convincing. Her first and final drafts are shown in Figure 6.16. She proofread her first draft and added some details as well as a grammatical correction. Then she asked her partner to

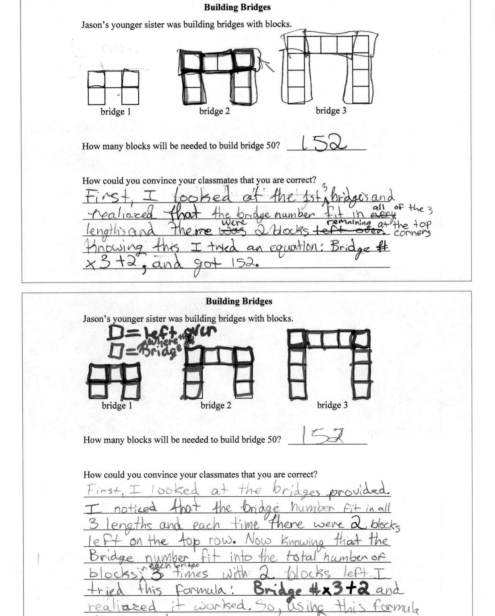

Figure 6.16
Erica's first and second drafts

read it and provide feedback. After reading it, her partner said, "This is good, but you need to tell more about how your work on the figures gets you to your formula." With labels and colors, Erica produced an explanation of which she was proud.

Justin became frustrated using the nonerasable felt-tip pens and switched to multilink cubes. He was trying to "see" how the bridges changed each time. Notice how his five original blue blocks (Figure 6.17) appear in each bridge, then the first set of three new blocks in yellow, and the next set in red. He had rebuilt his representation of bridge 3, with plans to insert three green blocks into it to represent bridge 4, when he exclaimed, "I've got it!" Justin hesitated a moment and then recorded his generalization 5 + 3 (bridge # − 1).

Figure 6.17
Justin's pattern built with cubes

Paisley found two different ways of looking at the growth of the bridges (Figure 6.18). Though her "formulas" related only to the fiftieth bridge, the structural elements she discovered would, I believe, allow her to determine the number of blocks for any bridge.

Philip saw the growing pattern in a way that was different from the thinking of others. His explanation provided the formula *(bridge # + 1) × (bridge # + 2) − bridge number × bridge number*. Looking back at the task shown in Figure 6.14, can you "see" his formula in the images?

Figure 6.18
*Paisley's two
ways of
thinking*

Building Bridges

Jason's younger sister was building bridges with blocks.

bridge 1   bridge 2   bridge 3

How many blocks will be needed to build bridge 50? 152 blocks

How could you convince your classmates that you are correct?

I know that the answer is 152 blocks because each bridge gets bigger by 3 blocks but the first bridge starts with 5 so you would add 2 to bridge 50.

My formula
(50 × 3) + 2 = 152/Bridge 50

Building Bridges

Jason's younger sister was building bridges with blocks.

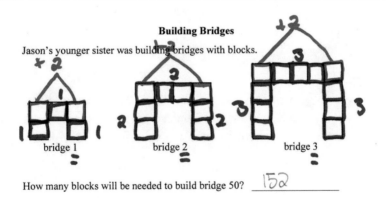

bridge 1   bridge 2   bridge 3

How many blocks will be needed to build bridge 50? 152

How could you convince your classmates that you are correct?

I know that there are 152 blocks in bridge 50 because in each bridge the colums and the length/top part have the same number of blocks as the bridge number and the corners are the +2.

My other Formula
(50 + 50 + 50) + 2 = 152 / bridge 50

Kathy's Reflection

I was surprised by how long students stayed engaged with this task. For seventy-five minutes, they made conjectures, tested their ideas, and wrote convincing arguments. They were fully involved in creating ways to convince others of their thinking. Their spontaneous use of color helped them and others follow their thinking. Next time, I might have students share their colorful representations of a given pattern and challenge others to write matching generalizations.

Several students wrote complete equations for their claims. Others provided only an expression. Some used A for their variable, because they thought about area, and others used I, standing for total number of blocks. There was an interesting conversation about the similarities and differences between Paisley's first approach and Justin's thinking. I loved listening to them figure out why Justin multiplied 3 by one less than the bridge number and Paisley multiplied 3 by the bridge number. During their group conversation, Lonnie's insight that "Justin started with 5, so he needed one less group of 3" really helped. I thought they all did a great job of listening carefully to each other and writing convincing arguments.

I Don't Agree!

There are a variety of ways in which we can stimulate classroom disagreements. One strategy that Angela Barlow and Michael McCrory suggest is giving students prompts that "force them to choose a side" (2011, 532). Here are some possibilities:

- ◆ Triangles are three-sided figures with a point at the top.
- ◆ A rectangle is a parallelogram.
- ◆ When you cut a rectangle to make its area smaller, its perimeter also gets smaller.
- ◆ All multiples of six are even numbers.
- ◆ All prime numbers are odd numbers.
- ◆ If the sum of the digits in a three-digit number is 8, the number is less than 710.

Such prompts can also give students the choice of responding *always true*, *sometimes true*, or *never true*. Many examples of these statements can be found at the following sites:

⇢ https://nrich.maths.org/12672

⇢ https://mathednerd.wordpress.com/always-sometimes-never/

⇢ https://kgmathminds.com/2014/11/26/always-sometimes-never-year-2/

Prompts can also be developed in response to classroom conversations.

Does the Turn-Around Rule Work for Subtraction?

In November, second-grade teacher Susan Speak considered the next lesson in the math text's section on subtraction. It was about turn-around facts (the commutative property) and whether it works in subtraction. In a recent professional development gathering, she had been part of a conversation with me and other educators from her district about thinking of the text as a resource, not a curriculum. Susan felt empowered by the discussion and decided that instead of following the prescribed lesson, she would have students investigate turn-around facts in addition and subtraction.

Susan had the students, in groups of two or three, respond by writing on large pieces of poster paper. Many students, such as Inez and Kara, decided that turn-around facts did not work with subtraction. But there were energetic disagreements. (See Figure 6.19.)

Figure 6.19
Students write about turn-around facts.

One group was adamant in its claim that it did work and gave examples of what they called double facts, such as $5 - 5 = 0$, to support their thinking. Others wondered about turning $3 + 4 = 7$ around to $7 - 4 = 3$. They discovered that they had different ideas about an example such as $2 - 4$. Some thought the answer was 2, some thought it was 0, and a few introduced negative numbers. Interest was high, and a few students even asked for indoor recess so they could continue to talk and write. Susan could not have been more pleased with their engagement.

As Mike Flynn writes, "One of the best things we can do for our students is give up some of our authority in math class" (2017, 80). So when the day ended, and the students turned to Susan to confirm what was right and wrong, she did not want to take their role as truth-finders away from them.

Instead, she congratulated them on their thinking and said that they would continue to learn about this idea. There were a few groans, but as Susan explained, "It wasn't the first time they had heard such a response from me. They know I don't give answers away."

Is Zero a Number?

Within a week, I overheard two conversations, one in grade two and one in grade four, in which a student casually said that zero was not a number. Both times, the conversation continued without the listener challenging the claim. I wanted to learn more about students' thinking about zero and how it changed as they got older. Kathy O'Connell Hopping offered to have students at her school respond to *I'm wondering . . . Is zero a number? Share your thinking.*

Kindergarten students were split in their opinions. Many students such as Andy and Lizzy justified their decisions by referring to zero's relationship to 1 (Figure 6.20). Two students who believed zero was a number made interesting comments. Jonas referred to zero as being in the middle on the number line, and Louisa dictated to her teacher that *It's like if you're not at school yet, it's zero. And then it is the first day of school.*

Figure 6.20
Andy's and Lizzy's kindergartner responses

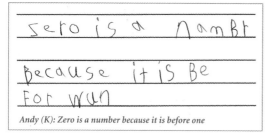

Andy (K): Zero is a number because it is before one

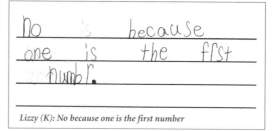

Lizzy (K): No because one is the first number

In first grade, more than one-third of the students claimed that zero was not a number. Harley referred to zero as nothing. Molly wrote about zero being part of other numbers, though she overestimated how often this happens. She also made her claim clear by ending her response with *yes*. Harley's and Molly's responses are shown in Figure 6.21.

In our informal survey, students' thinking changed dramatically in grades two through five. Though at each grade level two or three students did not believe zero was a number or wrote that it was *sort of* or *maybe* a number, the majority were clearly confident that it was. Both second and third graders mentioned the need for zeros to write numbers, and a few, such as Kamila, referred to its place between positive and negative numbers. As indicated by his phrase *What's hard about zero is*, Manny was less certain about zero's status. Kamila's and Manny's responses are shown in Figure 6.22.

Figure 6.21
Harley's and Molly's responses

0 is not a number because I 0 is like nothing. I think that like if like you say 10−0=10 is nothing.

Harley (grade 1): 0 is not a number because 0 is like nothing. I think that like if like you say 10 – 0 = 10 is nothing.

Share your thinking.

It is part of most nu-mbers. -10 -20 -30 -40 -50 -60 -70 -80 -90 -100 10 20 30 40 50 60 70 80 90 100 yes

Molly (grade 1): It is part of most numbers. -10 -20 -30 -40 -50 -60 -70 -80 -90 -100 10 20 30 40 50 60 70 80 90 100. Yes.

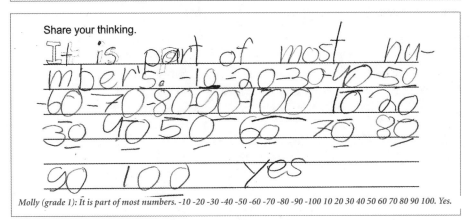

0 is a number because if you do an equason like 34+0=34, That includes 0 so it is a number. Also if it was not a number It would not seperate the negetives and the numbers So, it is a number.

$$100+0=100 \quad 100,000$$

$$10+0=20$$

Kamila (grade 3): 0 is a number because if you do an equation like 34 + 0 = 34, that includes 0. So it is a number. Also if it was not a number it would not separate the negatives and the numbers so it is a number.

You can use 0 to add and subtract. What's hard about zero is that it's not a number and is a number too! Zero represents a number so basicly what I think zero is a number. But if I hold up 3 fingers in one hand, and 5 inthe other, you know it's 8. But if I hold up 0 fingers, you'd say Zero or Nothing! So zero means nothing!

Manny (grade 2): You can use 0 to add and subtract. What's hard about zero is that it's not a number and is a number too! Zero represents a number so basically what I think zero is a number. But if I hold up 3 fingers in one hand, and 5 in the other, you know it's 8. But if I hold up 0 fingers, you'd say Zero or Nothing! So zero means nothing!

Figure 6.22
Kamila's and Manny's responses

In fourth grade, several students indicated that a value of zero is still a value, and that therefore, zero is a number. Dionice alluded to this as well as the relationship between zeros and multiples of ten. Fifth graders' responses demonstrated how their mathematical language, understanding of place value, and awareness of the ways we categorize numbers have developed. To communicate his thinking, Sam made a list of characteristics of zero. It included negative numbers, which he crossed out after the class discussion, in which he was convinced that zero was not negative. Dionice's and Sam's responses are shown in Figure 6.23. As mentioned earlier, a few students did not recognize zero as a number. One student, Arthur, focused on the idea that zero was a symbol but not a number.

Figure 6.23
Dionice's and Sam's responses

Zero is a number because 10 if the zero was not a number then 10 would only be one. A number has value zero also has value because 10+0 is still 10 the value of 0 is nothing. Zero is worth 10 times the number when pe it next to a number 10, 100, and 1,000. When ever you put a zero like this it always mutiplies it by 10. Zero still has value but the value is nothing, when it is add. When it is put with a number it mea rom multiply the before number by 10 then you have the answer for the next number. Like this...

10
10×10=
put a zero →100
100×10=
put a zero →1,000

The pattern then keeps on going

Dionice's response (grade 4)

Yes, Zero is a special number, a whole number, a digit, an integer and a rational number.

A Special Number:
• I and 0 are the only special numbers. There are many descriptions of a special number.

A Whole Number:
• A non-negitive number including 0

A digit:
• 0-9 including 0 and 9
• Used to form numbers

A Integer:
• Negative and non-negetive numbers
• All numbers

A Rational Number
• Any number that can be written as a fraction or ratio.

Sam's response (grade 5)

There is much we can learn from these responses, and, as mentioned in Chapter 3's discussion of what the equals sign means, looking at written work across grade levels can be profoundly informative. The teachers looked at this work and were surprised to find some similar ideas across several grade levels. I found it interesting that students were so clear about their opinions and that every classroom had its doubters.

Because so many students were writing about this idea, there was a certain buzz about it at the school. Some of the fourth graders were fascinated that kindergartners were responding to the same prompt they were. They asked Kathy if she would show them the kindergartners' work. The fourth graders were also surprised that some of the younger students' ideas were the same as their own. After some discussion about the similarities, David commented on the differences in the quality of their responses. He said, "I think it's a number, too, but I said it better. We need something to represent nothing, not just say that it is nothing."

Closing Thoughts

When students justify their thinking, rather than rely on a teacher or an answer key to determine the correctness of their ideas, they are developing their own sense of authority. Assessments often include an item or two that requires justification or the critique of others' thinking. But it's not about answering a question on a test; it's an approach to learning and thinking mathematically. If we want to build students' agency as mathematicians and their abilities to reason mathematically, they must be continuously engaged in interactive explorations in their classroom, working together to satisfy their own curiosities and discover their own sense of mathematical truth.

7 Writing to Connect Mathematics and Creativity

When I meet new people and they learn that I am a math educator, I often hear a groan, which is sometimes followed by a comment such as "I was always more into the creative subjects." To me, math is an exciting world of inquiry and discovery, where creativity plays an important role.

Inviting students to explore mathematical ideas through writing can break down the wall some perceive between math and creativity.

Writing Word Problems

"The creative writing of mathematical word problems is an invaluable tool for strengthening children's problem-solving skills" (Edwards, Maloy, and Anderson 2010, 347). Although asking students to write word problems is a common way we connect math to creative writing, it's still an infrequent request. Also, the opportunity to write their own problems is often included as one of several tasks for students to complete, rather than the focus of a lesson.

In early spring, Kathy O'Connell Hopping taught a lesson to third graders. The prescribed lesson in the text focused on two-step problems. After solving five word problems, the text directed students to write one of their own.

Instead, Kathy chose to make this last task the focus of the lesson. She provided two structures to help the students be successful. She gave them criteria for the number sentence the students were to create. It had to include

Figure 7.1
Word–problem–writing template

➡ either addition or subtraction and
➡ multiplication.

Number Sense	Picture
Brainstorm: What makes sense?	Word Problem

She also gave students a template (Figure 7.1) to complete and they used it, as a class, to create a two-step problem before students created problems on their own. They talked quite a bit about the *What makes sense?* section. Kathy explained that the numbers and context they chose should work together. She said, "If you started with 999, it wouldn't make sense for that number to represent how many cupcakes you ate last night." Because multiplication would be involved, they brainstormed sets of objects such as chairs in rows and pencils in boxes. When it came time for them to complete the task on their own, Kathy told them they could start with whichever one of the four sections they wished.

Most of the students started with either the number sentence or brainstorming sections, though two students began by making a picture. A group of three students, Adam, Bailey, and Hayden, worked while sitting close together. When Bailey wrote her number sentence, she shared it with the two boys, and they decided to write ones that were similar to hers but not exactly the same. Adam had recently been to the Central Park Zoo in New York City and loved the red pandas. He began with the brainstorming section and created a playful list (Figure 7.2). His chosen numbers were relatively small, though not small enough for the number of pandas likely to be given away. His number picture shows three groups of five as well as a representation of 1 ten regrouped to 10 ones. And, his pandas speak Spanish.

Bailey (Figure 7.3) drew a line to represent each group of ten stones, and she used *S* to stand for the number of funny-shaped stones she would keep for herself. She listed several small collections in her brainstormed list, which were appropriate, given that her numbers were less than or equal to one hundred. Notice that the clams would be found on a "small beach." Kathy asked her about a swim at the beach and Bailey enthusiastically explained, "I would want to swim one hundred times, maybe ten times each hour!"

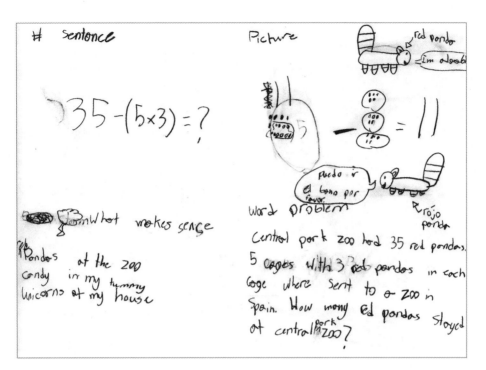

Figure 7.2
Adam's completed template

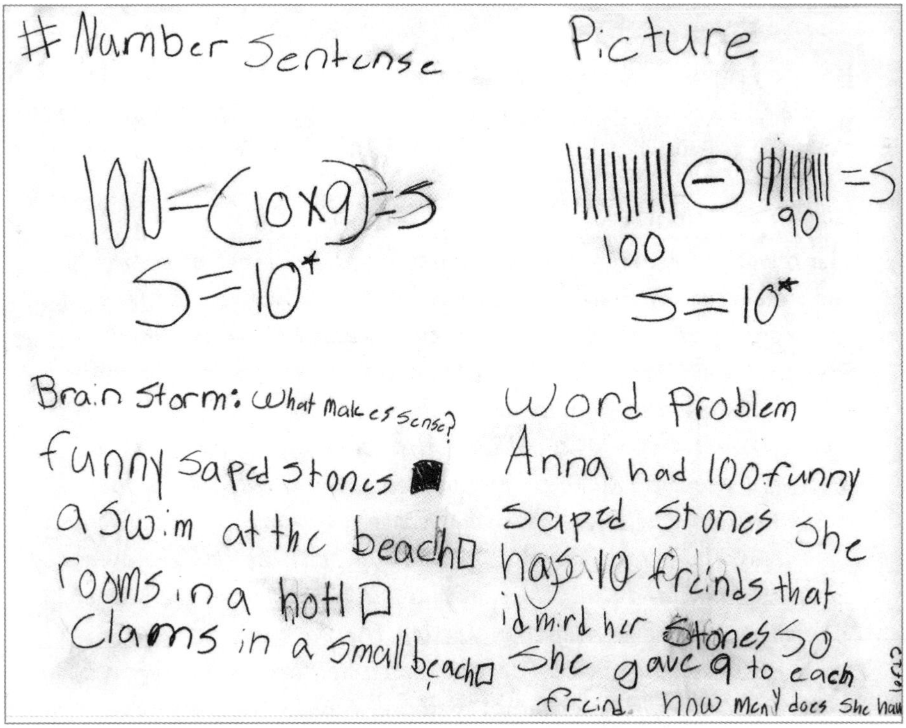

Figure 7.3
Bailey's completed template

Figure 7.4
Hayden's
completed
template

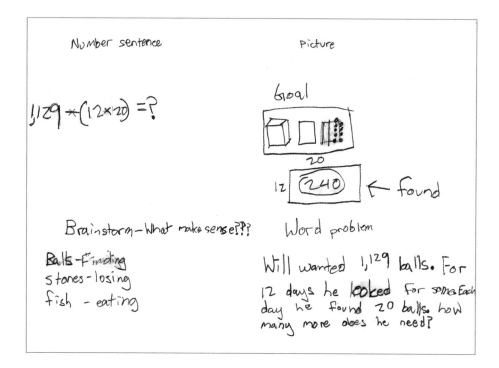

Hayden (Figure 7.4) used larger numbers and thus used base ten blocks in his picture and labeled his array, rather than drawing individual units. He also was the only student who chose to answer his question on the back of his paper.

Kathy's Reflection

The template really supported these students. Most of them chose the first item on their brainstormed list of what made sense, but I still think it was worth having them identify other possibilities. Students were excited about their problems and eager to share them with others. I would definitely teach the lesson this way again, though I think I would use the term _model_ rather than _picture_. I want to make sure students know I am looking for a visual representation, that an illustration would not be sufficient.

I found it interesting that this group of three students wanted to write equations that were similar but not exactly the same. When I asked them why they needed the parentheses, they told me, "Because you have to do the multiplication first." When they learn the order of operations, they will realize the parentheses are unnecessary, but for now, they have communicated their intent.

I worry sometimes about providing too much scaffolding for students, but this template gave just enough structure for them to weave together their thinking while providing an open-ended way to think about contexts for their problems. As they brainstormed ideas that they thought made sense, they combined creative thinking with sense making. Seeing how much they enjoyed this activity reminded me of the importance of tapping into a variety of ways for students to explore and share what they know.

Connections to Fiction

When we connect math to literature, we generate interest in mathematics while giving students a familiar context in which they can apply their mathematical thinking. There are many books with a strong and obvious connection to mathematics. One of my favorite classics is *Grandfather Tang's Story* by Ann Tompert (1990), which offers an interesting story, not one just to be read in connection with a math lesson. You probably have your own favorites.

Here are a few ways literature might be used to motivate creative writing about math. I mention specific titles, but if a book is unfamiliar to you, a simple online search will give you a synopsis that will help you identify one of your books that will work as well.

- **Retell a story** or part of a story by changing specific details but keeping the basic format intact. Stories such as *The Cookie Fiasco* by Dan Santat (2016), which is part of Mo Willems's Elephant and Piggy Like Reading! series, can begin with a different number of cookies and/or people. *Ten Times Better* by Richard Michelson (2000) could motivate students to write their own poems using a different relationship between numbers or with different real-world examples for single-digit numbers and those numbers times ten. Students could write their own versions of *Infinity and Me* by Kate Hosford (2012) by creating their own metaphors and/or asking friends and family how they imagine infinity.
- **Model a mentor text** by writing a similar book, but with different characters, focus, or setting. *Wild Ideas: Let Nature Inspire Your Thinking* by Elin Kelsey (2015) could motivate students to write a story about a student who learns how to solve math problems by watching strategies his or her classmates use. *The Button Box* by Margarette S. Reid (1990) could become *The Kitchen Junk Drawer* as students create their own book, perhaps adding tables to the format, that focuses on ways the items in a drawer could be sorted.

➡ **Create a sidebar character** to comment on the hidden mathematical content of the story. For example, consider *Goldilocks and the Three Bears* and a commentator with a fact-based persona that provides information such as *I imagine the child to be about six years old and about forty-two inches tall. So the right-sized chair would be* . . .

➡ **Build on a favorite character** and write related story problems. The problems don't have to relate to the specific story but can embrace a character's traits. Students might write problems related to the mischievous behavior of characters such as Pete the Cat or Matilda.

➡ **Change the ending** to a math book. Maybe the characters in *Two of Everything* by Lily Toy Hong (1993) would continue to duplicate until they formed their own country. How many duplications would that take?

The Day the _____ Quit

I also like to think about ways to link math to books that we wouldn't identify as having obvious connections to math. Near the end of the year I read *The Day the Crayons Quit* by Drew Daywalt (2013) to a class of second graders who had been studying the conventional format we use when writing letters. The book is about a boy named Duncan who opens his crayon box and finds a pile of correspondence, instead of crayons. With the exception of the letter from green, each crayon has written a complaint; for example, white is tired of being unseen, and gray is tired from drawing all the big animals that are gray, such as whales and hippos. The students clearly enjoyed this read-aloud. The whimsical illustrations by Oliver Jeffers and the feisty letters from the crayons inspired interest and conversation.

With student interest high, I told them we were going to think about a book that would be called *The Day the _____ Quit.* As I wrote this on the whiteboard, I told them it was going to be a math story and that their first task was to brainstorm what could go in the blank. Together, we made a list: shapes, numbers, math tools, and money. I then invited each of them to choose one of those words to put in the title and write a letter that would appear in that story. To support their prewriting, I gave students a template and suggested they spend a couple of minutes brainstorming with a partner before writing anything down. I enjoyed hearing them making decisions about the letters they were going to write. Figure 7.5 shows an example of a completed template.

As the students moved from planning to composing, their characters developed further and their author voices became stronger. Many of the students wrote to their mommy, daddy, or one of their teachers. Nicholai wrote to the U.S. Mint to tell it about the coins quitting because *nobody makes a dollar from us 100 pennies* and closed his letter, *your mistreated friend.* Bethany wrote to Mr.

Time because the clock was *getting tired of its hour hand that was so slow.* Carson's response was similar to many others. He identified a particular shape and then wrote about where we see circles and what will happen when they quit. Given his reference to balls and coins, he doesn't appear to distinguish between circle-shaped items and spheres. *I need a break!* captures the shapes' frustration.

Brooke wrote (Figure 7.7) from the perspective of a measuring tape that was angry about not being used and explained some of its advantages over a ruler: a tape can measure longer distances, measure things that are round, and fit in your pocket. Note how the strategic and repetitive use of exclamation points within the letter and *Grrrrrrr* help to effectively express the emotion she is trying to convey. I think this piece is remarkable for a second grader and shows a lot of sophisticated understanding about measurement, as well as creative writing.

My Planning Guide

What will quit: Clocks

How is clock used?	Why might ______ be angry?
to tell time write the time to no when to go places	because they are always used to tell time. they always stariing at it
What will happen when clocks quits?	**What do you need to remember about writing letters?**
nobody woul-d no what time it is	from, Dear,

Figure 7.5
Completed template

It's Mr Circle I am a shape, and in pictures I am a ball, coins and more I need a break! I feel over used in pictures if you dont give me a break, I will quit. You would need to make square heads, there would be no More circles and no more balls. your over used enimey, mr circle

Figure 7.6
Carson's letter

Dear Mommy
I quit! Nobody is using me! You could measure with me you could figure stuff out with me and, I'm very long. But you choose not to use me!! I just fee that I'm enemies with ruler I want to destroy him Because everybody wants to use him and not me!! Grrrrrr. If I quit you would have to use abou 10 rulers when you could use 1 of me, You can't measure something round with a ruler but you can with me, You cant fit a ruler in your pocket but since I go in a little box thing you can fit me in your pocket.
Your Friend, Tape Measurer

Figure 7.7
Brooke's letter

This lesson worked well; students were excited to write, and each conveyed a level of mathematical understanding I might not have noticed with a different type of activity. You could also use this activity in conjunction with a unit on measurement, shapes, or money to anchor student thinking in their newly acquired skills. Then the students could create a class book for everyone to enjoy.

Aimee's Books

Using model texts as part of writing workshop is common in today's classrooms. Sharing children's literature with students has always been one of Becky Eston Salemi's favorite aspects of teaching. Many years ago, she discovered *The Shape of Things* by Dayle Ann Dodds (1996). In the book, common shapes are connected to everyday objects. Phrases such as "A square is just a square until . . ." are repeated throughout the book, in this case, until a roof is added and it becomes a house. She has used this story, with its bold, crisp illustrations by Julie Lacome, ever since, when engaging her kindergarten students in an exploration of two-dimensional shapes. In December, she read the book and created anchor charts for circles, triangles, and squares so that students could consider the essential features of these basic shapes.

Near the end of the school year, Becky and Aimee met for a writing conference. Becky's goal was to check in on new pieces Aimee wanted to share. Since February, Aimee had really blossomed as a writer. Earlier, she had been timid about trying new topics. Her illustrations had been strong from the beginning, but she had been reluctant to add letters or words to tell her story. When Aimee pulled out two new books she wanted to share, Becky could see her confidence and eagerness. Their meeting began with the following conversation:

Becky: Tell me about your new books.
Aimee: I didn't have any more stories I wanted to write. I remembered a book about shapes. I liked when you read it.
Becky: Did that give you an idea?
Aimee: Yes. I found it in the shape books and then I made my own. I made a book about ovals. Then I made a book about a square.

Aimee proceeded to read her book *Ovals* (Figure 7.8) to Becky, followed by her book about a square that became the side of a basket for a hot air balloon. Later that day, Aimee read them to the class (Figure 7.9).

Ovals

An oval is just an oval until
You add a neck and a head

and four legs and a tail

and two ears and a mane.
You made a horse.

Figure 7.8
Aimee's book

Becky's Reflection

I found Aimee's story to be simple and elegant. In her own way, Aimee had used The Shape of Things as a model to write about something she loved. Throughout the year we had many conversations about her love for horses. Here she followed the idea of a model text used during math workshop to craft her own "how to draw a horse" book. It was a reminder for me that I never know when an idea will take hold, but that as a teacher, my job is to

Figure 7.9
Aimee prepares to read her stories to the class.

offer as many possible seeds for new thinking as I can. Outwardly I nodded for her to continue reading. Inwardly I bubbled over with joy at how much this clever child had grown and at her idea of writing a shape story.

As the author/illustrator of these books, Aimee had taken command of what she wanted to say. I believe she was driven by her desire to try something new. The model of <u>The Shape of Things</u> book had obviously stuck with her. You can see in each illustration how her pictures and words match. These are hallmarks of young writers that we try to foster. We also see her interest in shapes. Aimee's work shows us how writing and math can complement each other in support of the learner.

Literary Techniques

A mini-lesson in writing workshop might focus on a particular literary technique, and mathematics can be the context for using that technique.

Personification

Lina Lopez-Ryan and Jennifer Spencer were reviewing vocabulary words with their third-grade students. One of the follow-up choices they gave students was to pick two words and personify them by writing a conversation they might have. Kaine chose the words *multiplication* and *division* and wrote the dialogue shown in Figure 7.10. Notice how he alludes to the inverse relationship between multiplication and division and has identified their nicknames at the top of the page.

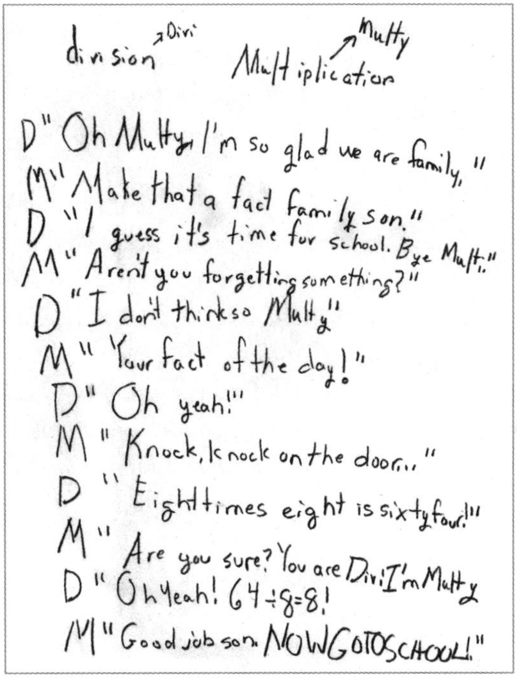
division → Divi Multiplication → Multy

D "Oh Multy, I'm so glad we are family."
M "Make that a fact family son."
D "I guess it's time for school. Bye Multi."
M "Aren't you forgetting something?"
D "I don't think so Multy."
M "Your fact of the day!"
D "Oh yeah!"
M "Knock, knock on the door..."
D "Eight times eight is sixty four!"
M "Are you sure? You are Divi I'm Multy
D "Oh Yeah! 64÷8=8!
M "Good job son. NOW GO TO SCHOOL!"

Figure 7.10
Kaine's conversation between Divi and Multy

RAFT is an acronym for role, audience, format, and topic and can be a tool for differentiating learning, because it provides students with choices. Fifth-grade teacher Lauren Gouzie created a RAFT (Figure 7.11) for her students that would require personification. She explained the format and told them they could choose the row they wanted for their writing.

Figure 7.11
RAFT directions

Role	Audience	Format	Topic
Decimal point	Digit in the thousandths place	Angry letter	Staying in the right place
Teacher	Student	How-to (with words and pictures)	Finding coordinates on the coordinate grid
X and Y coordinates	Student who mixes up their order	Helpful letter	Remembering the correct order

Lauren also created the following example to show students. She purposely chose a task not given as a choice so she wouldn't have too much influence on students' decision making.

R: Square
A: Geometry students
F: Persuasive letter
T: Why a square is the best shape

Dear math students who are CLEARLY studying the best area of math,
     I am here to explain to you why I, the amazing square, am the best shape in geometry. I stand for equality. My four sides are equal in length, and my four angles are equal, too. Not only are my angles equal, but they are also RIGHT angles. If it's not a right angle, it's a wrong angle, I always say! I am the best shape because I can be used in so many different areas of life; I can be used to form tiles, make cubes, and create blocks for stacking. I am the shape of all shapes. I am also the base of many shapes. Pull at my corners and angles and you can make a rhombus, a rectangle, and a parallelogram. There is only one shape that is the best, and that is me.
Signed,
The Amazing Square

Lauren's students thoroughly appreciated her persuasive letter and eagerly wrote their own versions. She told me that she couldn't believe how long her students wrote and how much they enjoyed sharing their work in small groups. Two samples are shown in Figure 7.12. Note the personality these students have incorporated into these letters. Both have included puns. Bri has offered *coordinating tips*, and Michelle has used *no point* twice in her story. Both are clear about their mathematical ideas and seem to have enjoyed the use of personification.

Exaggeration

When people tell or write stories, they sometimes use exaggeration to capture the interest of the audience. Fish are longer, crowds are bigger, and runners are faster. These exaggerations can add drama or humor to a story. Maureen O'Connell invited fourth-grade students to write a story with all of the numbers and measures exaggerated. She read them the following sentence to give them an idea of how the story might start: *I woke up this morning after sleeping for two years and discovered that I was $1\frac{1}{2}$ feet taller. That meant my bed was eighteen inches too short!*

Gretchen wrote a story about a guinea pig that grew twelve inches each day until it was *the size of her house and then up to the moon.* Lannie wrote about a birthday cake disaster with ingredients such as one cup of baking soda and five pounds of flour. For a further misfit, she added that she mixed them together in

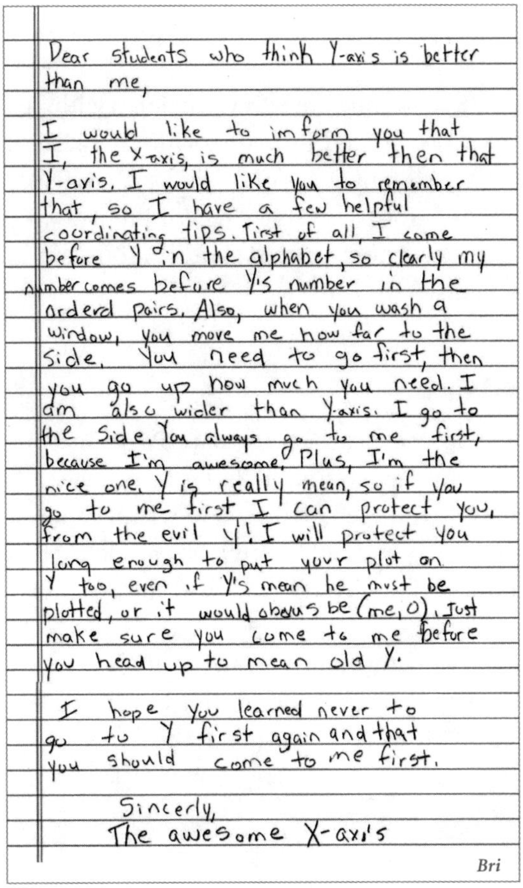

Dear students who think Y-axis is better than me,

I would like to imform you that I, the X axis, is much better then that Y-axis. I would like you to remember that, so I have a few helpful coordinating tips. First of all, I come before Y in the alphabet, so clearly my number comes before Y's number in the ordered pairs. Also, when you wash a window, you move me how far to the side. You need to go first, then you go up how much you need. I am also wider than Y-axis. I go to the side. You always go to me first, because I'm awesome! Plus, I'm the nice one. Y is really mean, so if you go to me first I can protect you, from the evil Y! I will protect you long enough to put your plot on Y too, even if Y's mean he must be plotted, or it would obveus be (me, 0). Just make sure you come to me before you head up to mean old Y.

I hope you learned never to go to Y first again and that you should come to me first.

    Sincerly,
    The awesome X-axis

Bri

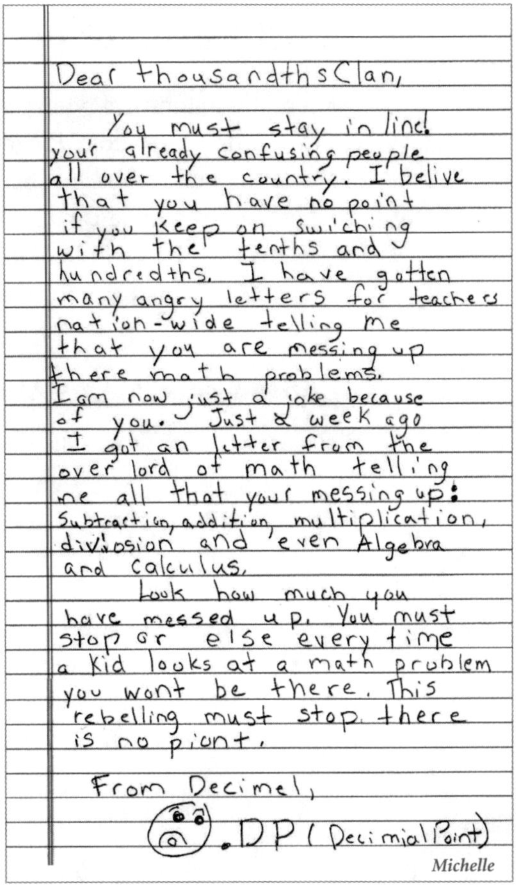

Dear thousandths Clan,

You must stay in line! you'r already confusing people all over the country. I belive that you have no point if you keep on swiching with the tenths and hundredths. I have gotten many angry letters for teachers nation-wide telling me that you are messing up there math problems. I am now just a joke because of you. Just a week ago I got an letter from the over lord of math telling me all that your messing up: Subtraction, addition, multiplication, division and even Algebra and calculus.

    Look how much you have messed up. You must stop or else every time a kid looks at a math problem you wont be there. This rebelling must stop. there is no piont.

    From Decimel,
    .DP (Decimial Point)

Michelle

Figure 7.12
Bri's and
Michelle's
letters

a measuring cup. As she wrote, she said, "We are doing something fun. I am messing with all my measuring units." We often emphasize the importance of units when we talk about measures. Notice how Frank captures their importance in his story titled "Weird" (Figure 7.13).

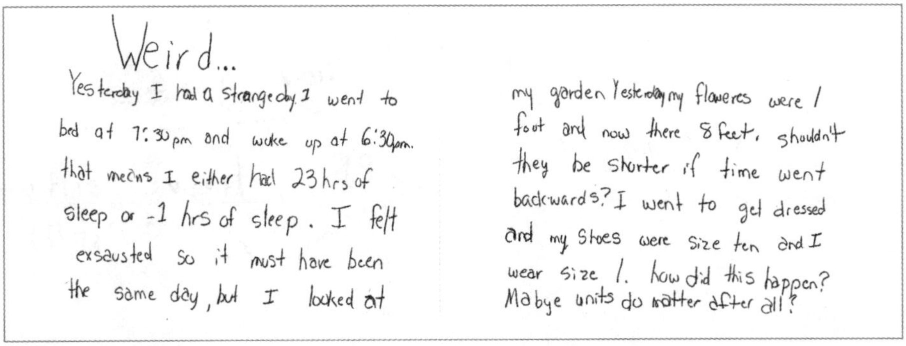

Figure 7.13
Frank's story

Weird...

Yesterday I had a strange day I went to bed at 7:30pm and woke up at 6:30pm. that means I either had 23 hrs of sleep or -1 hrs of sleep. I felt exsausted so it must have been the same day, but I looked at my garden Yesterday my flaveres were 1 foot and now there 8 feet. shouldn't they be shorter if time went backwards? I went to get dressed and my shoes were size ten and I wear size 1. how did this happen? Mabye units do matter after all?

Connections to Poetry

Both mathematics and poetry are able to communicate powerful ideas with just a few words or symbols. Poems can be connected to mathematics because of their content or because of their structure. Many types of poems, such as haiku or cinquain, require a certain number of words, syllables, and/or lines. Shapes of poems can also be important. Imagine writing a poem about a mountain in the shape of an equilateral triangle, pointed up.

Spontaneous Poems About Math

The Academy of American Poets encourages teachers to share Poem in Your Pocket Day with their students every April. Soon after Becky Eston Salemi's school celebrated this occasion, one of her kindergartners gave writing a math poem a try during writing workshop. Becky did not realize Ava was doing this until Ava came over to Becky and asked if she could read it to the class. Her poem is shown in Figure 7.14.

When Ava read her poem to the class, many of her classmates applauded. As is the practice in Becky's class, Ava asked her classmates if they had any questions or comments. One student asked, "How did you think of this?"

Figure 7.14
Ava's math poem

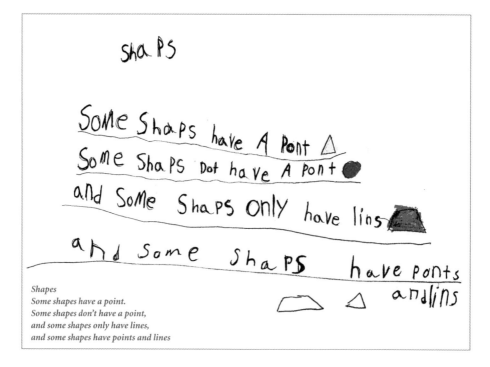

Shapes
Some shapes have a point.
Some shapes don't have a point,
and some shapes only have lines,
and some shapes have points and lines

Ava replied, "I like shapes, and I wanted to write a poem, so I wrote about the details like we do when we write stories."

Another student commented, "I like how you had the circle. It has no points." Ava beamed.

Though Becky was aware that mathematically, the information in Ava's poem is not 100 percent accurate and that some folks might argue that it isn't a poem, she was also mindful of the joy this brought to Ava and her classmates. Also, Ava's willingness to share her mathematical ideas through poetry encouraged others to do the same. In fact, Becky shared this piece with Pia, a fifth grader, who then wrote her own math-inspired poem (Figure 7.15).

Do you hear the power of Pia's voice and how it builds from "meaningless" to "mysteries"? Isn't this our goal for all students? Becky's heart leapt as she thought about this student sharing her understanding and love of mathematics that built to the powerful crescendo "and victories in MATH!"

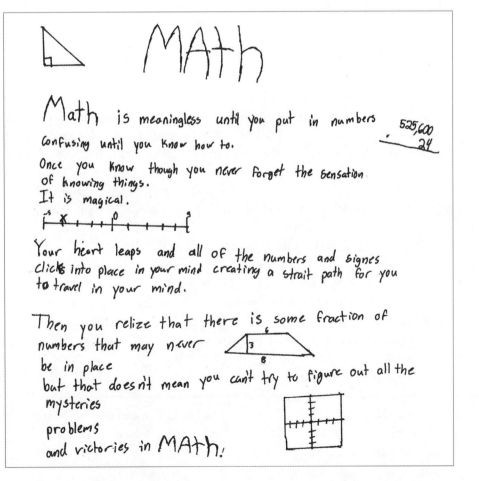

Figure 7.15
Pia's poem

Structured Math Poems

My favorite structure for a mathematical poem is a dialogue poem or what Theoni Pappas (1993) calls a poem for two voices. To create such a poem, two authors identify two related but different things or ideas, such as addition and subtraction. Then, "Similarities and differences between concepts can be explored, giving the rhythm and the feel of a dialogue" (Dacey and Donovan 2013, 144). I like to have students write in columns, one for each voice, ending with a line that identifies something that is true for both voices. I wrote the following example for Kathy O'Connell Hopping to share with a class of fourth graders just finishing a poetry unit.

Triangle	*Rectangle*
Three sides	*Four sides*
Equilateral triangles	*Squares*
Tortilla chips, sails, yield signs	*Graham crackers, doors, books*
Tetrahedron	*Rectangular prism*

We are both polygons.

Kathy invited two students to read the poem, which was projected on the whiteboard. She explained that the readers would alternate, one reading the triangle lines and one the rectangle lines. The last line, written in the middle, would be read by both of them. These simple poems always seem more meaningful when read aloud; it can feel as if you've been invited to listen to a private conversation.

After the reading, Kathy asked the students to read the poem again, silently, and then share what they noticed. They made the following comments:

Seamus: I noticed that the lines go together.
Rachel: I noticed that one line is about where we see those shapes.
Dan: I noticed that the first example was food.
Janifer: I noticed that their three-dimensional shapes were named.
Arco: I didn't get the part about equilateral triangles and squares.
Mimi: I didn't either, at first, but then I got that it's because the sides are all the same.
Arco: Oh, I get it now.

Next, Kathy explained that they were going to work in pairs to write their own poems. They talked briefly about "topics" that would make sense. Their ideas included some of the following:

- multiplication and division
- perimeter and area
- decimals and fractions
- numerator and denominator
- inch and foot
- penny and dollar

Kathy encouraged students to decide the identity of each voice and then brainstorm ideas.

Alex and Viola choose to write a poem (Figure 7.16) about decimal and fraction. Many of their lines have the same number of words and syllables, giving the poem rhythm. They also included a near rhyme with *line* and *time*. After they read their poem aloud, students asked about the eye and mouth. Viola giggled and explained that the word *decimal* has the letter *i* in it, and that they thought the *c* in *fraction* looked like a mouth.

Sebastian and Dagon wrote a poem about multiplication and division. When they finished, Sebastian said, "I like these. We can just talk and we get a poem." Dagon shared his enthusiasm, and they decided to write another poem. They turned their paper over, made a chart, and wrote about acute and obtuse (Figure 7.17).

I had purposely included real-world examples in the model poem, and these students did as well. It's important for students to make such connections, and having examples from students themselves is much better than using pictures in a textbook. Kathy told me the students enjoyed writing and listening to

Figure 7.16
Alex and
Viola's poem

Your topics: Decimal + fraction	
Vocie 1 - Decimal	Voice 2 - fraction
Has a dot	Has a line
Side to side	Up and down
On the stop watch	Half time!
have an eye	have a mouth
0.25	$\frac{1}{4}$
Were both part of a number	

Figure 7.17
Sebastian
and Dagon's
poem

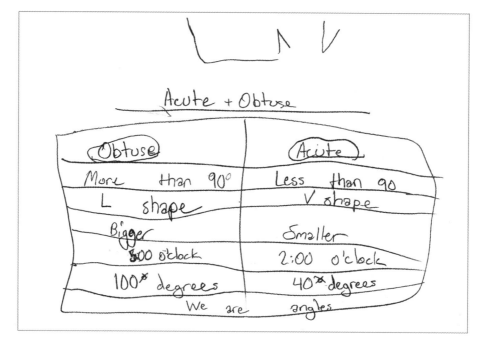

these poems, and that the fourth-grade teachers decided that next year, they would include this idea in their poetry unit. You can also explore these poems as a call-and-response routine, with you (or a student) offering a line and the class (or another student) responding. You also might want to consider a math poetry slam focused on dialogue poems.

Closing Thoughts

When we give students the opportunity to explore creative ways to write about math, we integrate learning and increase student involvement. We get a view of our students' thinking from a different perspective. When we include creative and poetic writing as ways to think about math, we can blend math and writing workshop time. Most important, with this form of writing we increase the likelihood that creativity and math will be thought of as a plausible combination, with numerous learning opportunities.

8 Writing to Reflect

When students have time to reflect on their learning, they often make new connections or may recognize and resolve their confusion. They're able to develop the ability to self-monitor and foster responsibility for their own learning. Reflecting through writing is particularly helpful because it allows students the space to focus without distractions.

It's important for students—and teachers—to stop and capture their thinking, so it's important that we not move on too quickly to the next lesson or activity. Writing reflections causes us to pause and allows ideas to sink in and deepen. In this chapter, we will consider how to structure student reflections about what they notice, what is not correct, how they prefer to work, which tools or strategies they prefer to use, and how they've changed over time.

Journals, Math Notebooks, and Learning Logs

"The use of journals in math classes provides students a tool to record their personal learning" (Kostos and Shin 2010, 225). Today, many educators use the terms *journals, math notebooks,* and *learning logs* interchangeably. For some, journals are a place for writing after an event or lesson, logs are for documenting thinking and observations during investigations, and math notebooks are considered all-purpose. Of course, it doesn't matter what they are called. What's important is that students have a place to write about their thinking, and it is helpful if this type of writing is kept together, so it can be reviewed at a later time.

Kristen Gray, a K–5 math specialist as well as a Teaching Channel Laureate, is an expert at having students write in journals. You can read about students' use of them in her blog at https://kgmathminds.com/. Kristen also encourages teachers to keep a personal math journal. Taking the time to chronicle the twists and turns of a lesson or the discovery of a student's partial or advanced understanding can help us better understand learning trajectories and where our students fall on them. Writing reflectively can also help us home in on the essential elements of a lesson, unveiling pitfalls, plateaus, and positive outcomes of our instruction.

Recently, Jennifer Spencer and Lina Lopez-Ryan included math notebooks in their third-grade classroom for the first time, and I had the pleasure of observing their use. Students were exploring a number story. Some students were using linking cubes, some were talking in pairs about how to best approach the task, and some were trying different strategies on scrap paper. It was interesting to see notebooks emerge naturally when students were ready to write about what they had discovered on their own or with a partner. It was as natural a process as taking out a ruler to draw a straight line.

In this class, students use the notebooks for many types of writing. They record what they notice and wonder, reflect on their understanding of concepts and ideas, and write creatively. Sometimes they write a summary of something that stood out for them in a lesson. For instance, Thomas wrote, "I learned that parallel sides are two lines that can go straight forever but still be the same distance apart as how they started." Sometimes students pose questions. One of my favorites was the insightful, "I am still a little confused about division. What would happen if you had extra?"

Both Jennifer and Lina have been very excited about how the notebooks have transformed their math teaching. Lina said, "It's amazing how positive the students are about writing in math." Jennifer added, "The students have become attached to their notebooks, and so have we." In fact, a couple of times during the year, they each mentioned to me that they were reluctant to let the students take their notebooks home with them at the end of the year. They wanted to take the summer to reread them, to reflect together on how the notebooks had supported learning.

Two weeks before the end of school, I received an email from Jennifer in which she wrote, "Something magical happened yesterday in our math class. I so wish we had captured it on video." She went on to explain that when she and Lina announced that they wanted to continue to learn from the notebooks over the summer and that students could retrieve them in the fall, students spontaneously started saying heartfelt goodbyes to their notebooks. Some whispered, "I'll miss you," and others handed them over after a hug or gentle pat on the cover. Hoping to balance the loss and encourage a lifelong habit of writing about their curiosities and what they found meaningful, Jen and Lina bought the students new math notebooks for summer use. During the last week of school, students spent time creating and planning for math ideas they would explore during July and August. A brainstorming session led to student-generated outdoor activities such as timing how fast they could swim to the dock, charting different types of vehicles as they passed on their streets, and measuring how close they could get to a squirrel.

Noticing

Reflection helps students gain and link significant insights from their experiences (Costa and Kallick 2008). Merely asking students what they notice gives them a moment to step back and contemplate what they have just seen or heard. Asking them to record what they notice suggests this thinking is not fleeting or trivial, and helps students clarify it further.

After Playing Games

Becky Eston Salemi's kindergarten students had been playing a variety of games designed for practice of addition. By the end of the school year, the app Math Tappers: Find Sums by Tim Pelton had become a favorite. You can find this free app at https://itunes.apple.com/us/app/mathtappers-find-sums-math-game-to-help-children-learn/id353582286?mt=8. The game asks students to choose a target number (sum) and then to choose two number cards (addends) to create that sum. Those number cards are then removed and students try to find another combination for that target, using the cards that remain. To play, students worked individually on an iPad.

Very quickly, Finding Sums became the focus of a lot of math talk. Students were comparing what they noticed by making comments such as "I did that one; it didn't have very many," or "That one was easy for me. How do I change the number?" When Becky started to hear these exchanges, she decided to investigate further. She quickly realized that some students were watching while others played the game. There are enough iPads to set up a small-group station as one of the choices during math workshop, but not enough for all students. Becky encourages students not to waste their time waiting for a chance to use them, and was about to suggest they choose a different activity when she heard an observer comment, "There won't be many for that number." Becky reacted quickly, to take advantage of what was happening, and offered them the opportunity to write about what they were noticing. Students eagerly switched gears and brought blank paper and pencils over to the center. They recorded what they noticed, using their stance as both observers and players to generate reflective and insightful ideas.

Becky was delighted with the range in student responses and the ideas they recorded. How impressive that these five- and six-year-olds noticed that the higher the sum, the more possibilities there are for adding two numbers (addends) to equal that target number (sum). Almost all students ended up writing something about this idea. Rex's response is shown in Figure 8.1.

A few students had other ideas. When Becky first read Penelope's work (Figure 8.2), only the first part was on her paper. Becky was struck by what Penelope had written, but was not 100 percent sure what she meant, and asked for clarification. Penelope was hesitant at first, but when Becky encouraged her to make her idea more complete, Penelope added the second part. Becky was expecting Penelope to write about how she noticed that the target number is not among the choices given, but was surprised by the additional and insightful statement that zero was also not included.

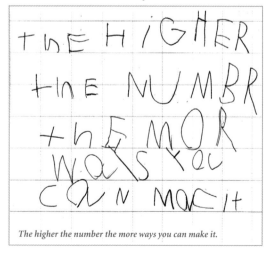

Figure 8.1
What Rex noticed about the game

The higher the number the more ways you can make it.

Figure 8.2
What Penelope noticed about the game

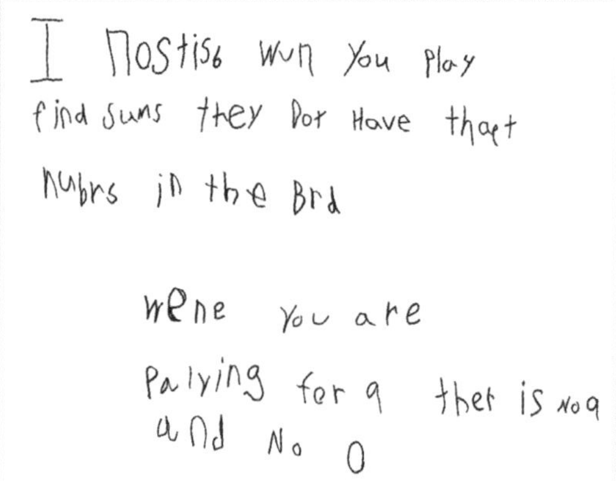

I noticed when you play Find Sums they don't have that number in the board.
When you are playing for nine, there is no nine and no zero.

After a Lesson

Jennifer Spencer and Lina Lopez-Ryan sometimes bridge lessons for their third graders by asking them at the start of the second lesson to write about what they did the day before and identify something they noticed. On the day after students had created fraction strips, Jen and Lina wanted them to activate prior learning before beginning the second lesson, in which they would use the strips to compare fractions. Third grader Will's response is shown in Figure 8.3. Will recalled this information himself, through his reflective writing; it is likely to

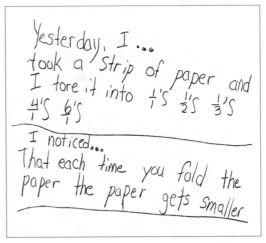

Figure 8.3
Will's reflection on yesterday's lesson

be more meaningful to him than it would have been if his teachers had simply begun this class meeting by summarizing the previous lesson. Because this was the first instance this year that fractions were considered, it's not surprising that he reversed the numerators and denominators in his recording of one-fourth and one-sixth.

Students can also write about a lesson just after it has ended. Lina and Jen have students use the categories *stranger, acquaintance,* and *friend* to sort vocabulary words and math facts. After some work with division, Maddox used two of these words to capture his response to the lesson. His reflective comment is shown in Figure 8.4.

I think division was an acquaintance but now it's a friend

Figure 8.4
Maddox's comment after a lesson on division

Self-Correcting

One of the important ways in which students can take ownership of their thinking and learning is to self-correct. When mistakes are accepted as important aspects of the learning process, they can be recognized as opportunities. Sometimes we ask students to reflect on partial understandings; sometimes they spontaneously want to write about an error they have made.

Something's Wrong

Kathy O'Connell Hopping showed fourth graders a number line marked with the numbers one and one million. She asked students to indicate where one thousand would be on this number line, and to tell how they decided where it should be placed. Celina seemed a bit agitated when she gave Kathy her paper. She said, "Something's not right. I need to think about this more." Because it was the end of the day, Kathy encouraged Celina to do that and assured her they could talk about it the next day.

When Kathy looked at Celina's response (Figure 8.5), she noticed Celina had associated these numbers with base ten blocks. With the exception of ten, which she omitted, she marked each of the powers of ten between one and one million. Because she had created the same amount of space between each number she recorded, Kathy wondered if Celina thought that the difference between one hundred and one thousand was the same as that between one thousand and ten thousand. This idea is subtly reinforced in place-value charts that show the places right beside each other, as if the distance between one and ten is the same as between ten and a hundred. You might want to look around your school and see if there are any proportional number line models of the powers of ten.

Figure 8.5
Celina's number line

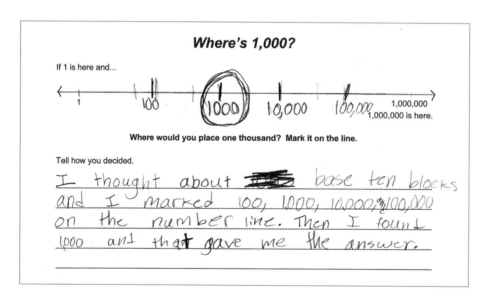

As soon as Celina arrived at school the next day, she looked for Kathy. When they met, Celina announced, "I thought about it and have a new idea." Kathy suggested that Celina write down her new thinking for Kathy to look at when she came to the classroom later that day. When they had talked the day before,

Kathy wasn't sure that Celina would hold on to this concern about her thinking. She knew that students' priorities often change once the school day has ended, but Celina had clearly remained interested in this task, and Kathy was eager to read about her updated thinking.

In her reflection (Figure 8.6), Celina wrote that she remembered placing one thousand in about the middle of the number line, but that half of a million was five hundred thousand, not one thousand. On the back of her sheet, she drew the correct placement. Kathy said that Celina was bothered by her initial response, but was calm and confident after writing about her new thinking.

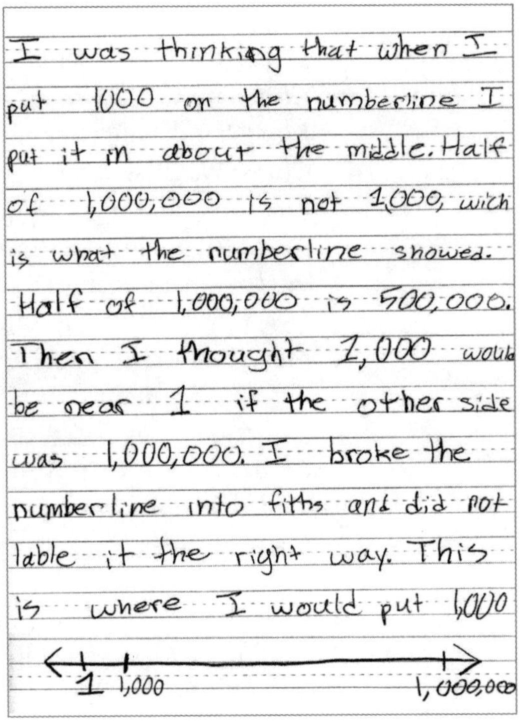

I was thinking that when I put 1000 on the numberline I put it in about the middle. Half of 1,000,000 is not 1,000, wich is what the numberline showed. Half of 1,000,000 is 500,000. Then I thought 1,000 would be near 1 if the other side was 1,000,000. I broke the numberline into fiths and did not lable it the right way. This is where I would put 1,000

Figure 8.6 Celina's thoughts the next day

Celina has high standards, so it isn't surprising that she felt unsatisfied with her response. Her willingness to stick with this task may also have been influenced by the conversations in her class about the importance of mistakes and how they provide opportunities for learning. It may also be that Celina was on the edge of understanding and this prompt arrived at exactly the right time. Regardless, the fact that she recorded her ideas allowed her to consider them again and draw a new conclusion.

What We Forgot to Do

I gave fifth graders the following task:

> *Tanya has only nickels and quarters in her jar.*
> *She has 13 times as many nickels as quarters.*
> *She has $8.10 in her jar.*
> *How many quarters does Tanya have?*

The students were familiar with using a guess-and-check strategy, and most found a solution within five guesses, during which time they had important conversations about whether their next guess should be higher or lower. I noticed that Justin and Chloe were struggling. I sat by them, and we had the following conversation:

Me: How's it going?

Justin: Not well at all.

Chloe: We've made so many guesses. It just doesn't work.

Me: Tell me about your guesses and what you did with them.

Chloe: We guessed for nickels and then got the quarters.

Me: How did you get the quarters?

Chloe: We multiply by thirteen.

Justin: That's what it says. (Justin points to the second line in the problem as he makes this comment.)

Me: (Pause) Then what happens?

Justin: We multiply the nickels by five to find their value. And, wait, wait, I mean . . .

Chloe: Wait, that's it. We didn't multiply the quarters.

Justin: Wow.

Chloe and Justin returned to the task and found a solution within a few guesses.

When I assigned the problem, I let students know that once they found their solution, they would write to reflect on one of the following questions:

- What are you most proud of today?
- How did you organize your thinking as you explored the problem?
- What challenged you as you solved the problem?

I told them they could write individually or with their partner.

Chloe said, "I'm going with the third one. I need to write about what happened to us." (See Figure 8.7.) Note that she didn't suggest that the problem was too challenging or tricky; rather, she took responsibility for their inability to find an answer easily and said what she could do next time. It seemed to me that this writing brought Chloe closure and gave her a sense that she could keep this from happening again.

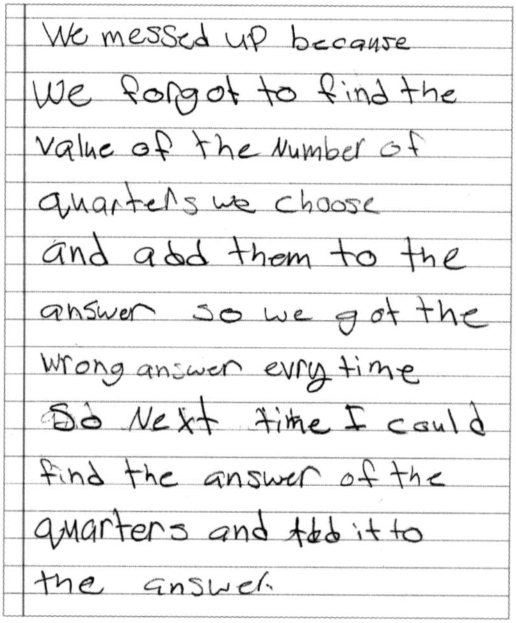

> We messed up because we forgot to find the value of the Number of quarters we choose and add them to the answer so we got the wrong answer evry time So Next time I could find the answer of the quarters and add it to the answer.

Figure 8.7
Chloe's reflection

How to Work

This year, math coach Jayne Bamford Lynch was assigned to coach her school's Olympiad team. She invited all students in grades four and five to join. A group of fifteen students participated, nine of whom showed up every Wednesday morning before school to solve math problems. They wanted to feel as if they were in a club, so they had T-shirts made (see Figure 8.8). They designed the logo by collecting data about their favorite numbers and those of their coaches and teachers. They included the symbol for infinity to express that they would work hard forever.

Figure 8.8
T-shirt designed by the students

The group included a few students with individualized education plans and one student who suffered from high anxiety. Jayne decided that giving too much attention to competition and speed would not work with this group, so she awarded them three times as many points for every problem they solved correctly while working together. Jayne said that in the fall, they basically said no thank you to anything that was challenging, but that over time, they discovered that they could each contribute, in some way, to a group trying to solve a problem.

As it came time for the competition in the spring, Jayne began to worry. How would these students feel when they compared themselves to other teams? As part of their preparation, she had them reflect on whether they liked to work best in a team or independently. Chandra reported that she liked working in a group better. She wrote about how you could think of more ideas when you worked with others and also mentioned that when you build a house, you do it in a group (Figure 8.9).

> I liked working with working with a groop better than working indipendently, because, ways that you can think of more so you can solve the problems you have more ideas of how to do it. Some times you can only think more of one way to do it, if you have help. Like when bilding a house you can have more than one idea and make the house stabler, pluse you don't bild a house by Yourself you do it with a groop.

Figure 8.9
Chandra's reasons for wanting to work in a group

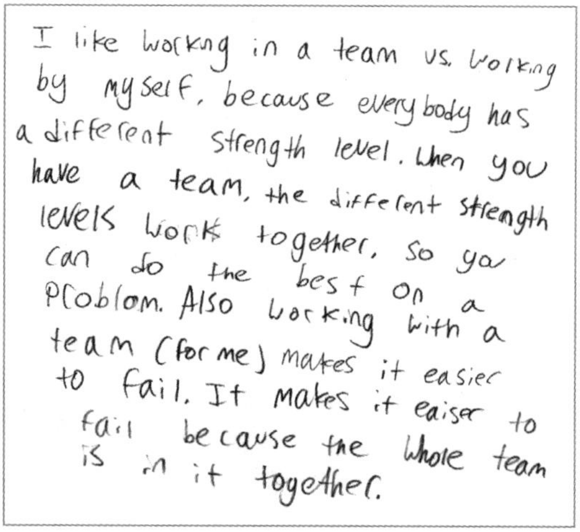

Figure 8.10
Deanna's preference to work on a team

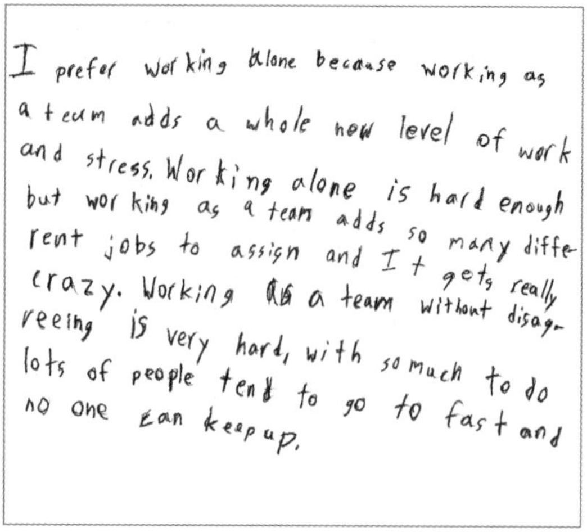

I like working in a team vs. working by myself, because everybody has a different strength level. When you have a team, the different strength levels work together, so you can do the best on a problem. Also working with a team (for me) makes it easier to fail. It makes it eaiser to fail because the whole team is in it together.

Figure 8.11
Hudson's reasons for wanting to work alone

I prefer working alone because working as a team adds a whole new level of work and stress. Working alone is hard enough but working as a team adds so many different jobs to assign and it gets really crazy. Working as a team without disagreeing is very hard, with so much to do lots of people tend to go to fast and no one can keep up.

Deanna also liked to work as part of a team (Figure 8.10). Her reasons included the different strength levels of the members of the group. She wrote poignantly about failure. She claimed that working with a team *makes it easier to fail, because the whole team is in it together.* She also shows insight by recognizing that although this was true for her, it may not be for everyone.

Hudson wrote that he would rather work alone and gives multiple reasons for this preference (Figure 8.11). He believes that teamwork increases the amount of work and stress involved. It appears he also believes it's hard for people to work together without having disagreements and that some will work too fast, leaving others behind.

Jayne's Reflection

I wanted to learn more about what these students thought about working together, but mostly I wanted them to hear about each other's preferences. I invited them to share what they wrote, and several of them did. As I suspected, revealing their thinking about working together brought them closer. Hudson told Deanna that even though he preferred to work alone, he liked the part she wrote about them failing together. Fiona told Hudson to tell the team members if he needed them to slow down. I'm glad I had them write rather than turn and talk. It gave them more time for reflection and helped them remember their own ideas after they listened to someone else's.

The first part of the competition was individual, and as I expected, most of the students did not receive high scores, but they worked hard and handled it well. Once they were able to work as a team, they did much, much better. I was happy for them and could tell they were proud of their accomplishments. I will invite all fourth and fifth graders to join next year as well. It's really important that all students be encouraged to participate. These students have grown more confident, and their problem-solving abilities are stronger. They have also realized that their teammates can hear and respect their preferences.

Which Would You Rather Use?

Analyzing how things are the same or different is an important aspect of critical thinking, and research indicates that students achieve more when they are involved in comparative thinking (Marzano 2007; Marzano, Pickering, and Pollock 2001). Making comparisons involves reflective thinking because it asks students to link and evaluate ideas and experiences. In math, students can compare strategies, solutions, tools, and concepts. They could compare the following:

- a number line and a hundreds chart;
- counting by ones and counting by twos;
- a ruler and a meter stick;
- a clock and a ruler;
- two bar graphs with the same labels but different data;
- a digital clock and an analog (face) clock;
- addition and subtraction or multiplication and division;
- specific strategies for finding a sum (difference, product, or quotient);
- charts and Venn diagrams; and
- fractions and decimals.

Which Strategy?

Metacognitive skills include knowing different strategies and when to use them (Baker 2012). Jayne Bamford Lynch asked a small group of second-grade students to find the answer to $342 - 189$ and then write why they chose the strategy they used. She wanted students to be aware of the choices they were making and to share them with one another. Jayne knows that when students reflect on the use of different strategies, they become more mindful of why one might be a better choice than another. This focus is different from explaining how a strategy was used or justifying its use and may generate particularly powerful writing when students are in the process of learning new strategies.

Kelsey chose to use an open number line to find the distance between the two numbers. Though she did not indicate direction by including arrows, she actually found the difference by adding up, starting at 189. Notice her attention to benchmark numbers. She added 100 first, and then added 11 more to land on 300. She explained (Figure 8.12) that the number line was easier to use because *you don't have to keep regrouping.* Her clarity about why she preferred the number line may allow her to use a different strategy when no regrouping is required. Note her reference to *an up and down equation.* What a wonderful way to connect the way we write an equation with the way we write numbers when using the standard algorithm.

Robert chose to subtract by parts (Figure 8.13). He is not finding the distance between the two numbers, but rather, taking 189 from 342. Notice how he focused on subtracting multiples of ten or subtracting numbers to reach a multiple of ten.

In his reflection, Robert explained that breaking the numbers into smaller pieces was easier for him (Figure 8.14). Jayne wanted students to reflect on why they used a particular strategy because she thought other students would pay

Figure 8.12
Kelsey's strategy and reflection on what makes a number line easier to use

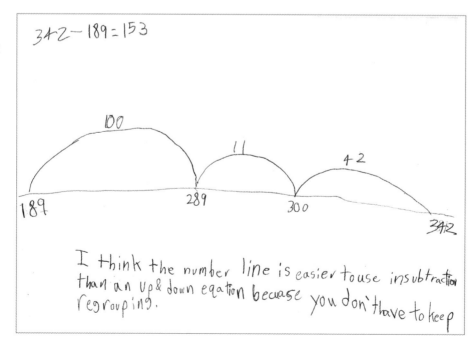

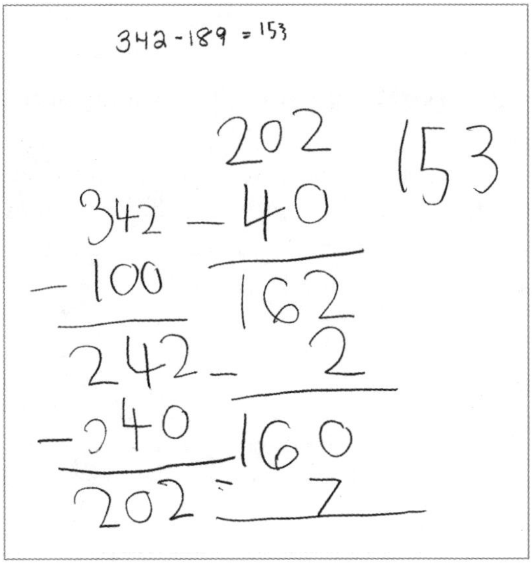

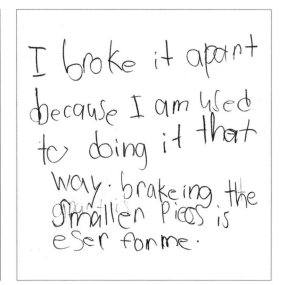

Figure 8.13
Robert's work showing subtraction by parts

Figure 8.14
Robert's reflection on his strategy

close attention to their classmates' preferred choices. They did. Jayne said students listened carefully to each other's ideas and asked questions about the work that was recorded. For example, a classmate, Brian, asked Robert, "How do you decide where to break the numbers?"

Lists or Venn diagrams, Fractions or Decimals

Kathy O'Connell Hopping asked a small group of fifth-grade students to compare fractions and decimals. She told them they could choose to complete a same/difference chart or a Venn diagram to organize their thinking. Students had used both tools in literacy learning. After their ideas were recorded, they discussed their findings. Because students had spent time thinking about and recording their ideas, it was a lively discussion. Kathy found it to be an excellent way to uncover, review, and solidify ideas related to fractions and decimals.

Next, Kathy asked them to write in response to one of these two reflective questions:

- *Which one did you use to organize your thinking: a same/difference chart or a Venn diagram? Why?*
- *Is it easier to work with fractions or decimals? Or is it the same for you?*

Originally, several students chose to complete a chart, though all but Ned switched to a Venn diagram. Ned's chart is shown in Figure 8.15. Notice that by subdividing the difference column, he has created the same three sections available inside the two rings of a Venn diagram.

His reflective writing (Figure 8.16) suggests that space is the major reason Ned chose this format. He also indicated that this is a common choice for him when he wrote, *I personally like charts in all of my writing.* Interestingly, he told the group, "I didn't realize I used charts so much until I wrote this."

Figure 8.15
Ned's chart

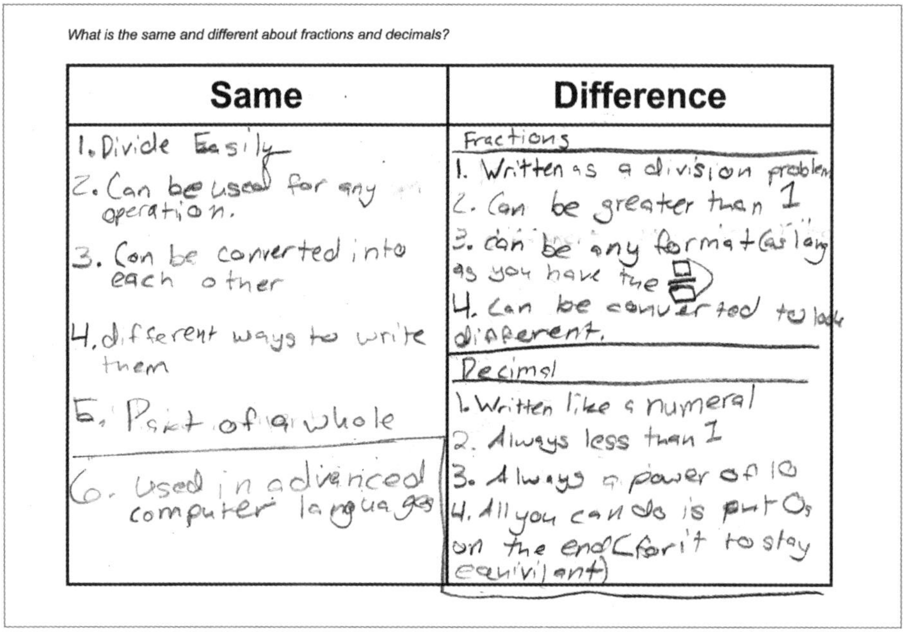

What is the same and different about fractions and decimals?

Same	Difference
1. Divide Easily	Fractions
2. Can be used for any operation.	1. Written as a division problem
3. Can be converted into each other	2. Can be greater than 1
4. different ways to write them	3. can be any format (as long as you have the ▢)
5. Part of a whole	4. Can be converted to look different.
6. Used in advanced computer language	Decimals
	1. Written like a numeral
	2. Always less than 1
	3. Always a power of 10
	4. All you can do is put 0s on the end (for it to stay equivilant)

Figure 8.16
Ned's reflection on why he chose to use the chart

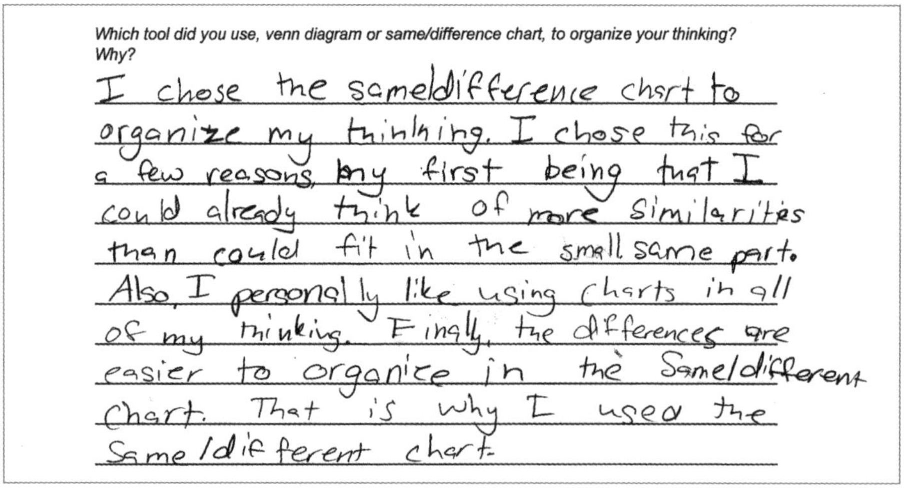

Which tool did you use, venn diagram or same/difference chart, to organize your thinking? Why?

I chose the same/difference chart to organize my thinking. I chose this for a few reasons, my first being that I could already think of more similarities than could fit in the small same part. Also, I personally like using charts in all of my thinking. Finally, the differences are easier to organize in the Same/different chart. That is why I used the Same/different chart.

Kim used a Venn diagram (Figure 8.17). It clearly shows how many common aspects of fractions and decimals she recognized. Her generalizations about how multiplication and division change the size of fractions and decimals were unique. Like a few other students, she listed that they were both used in computer programming languages. She has been learning about coding through the school's STEM initiative.

Space also contributed to Kim's decision about which format to use. She wrote in her reflection (Figure 8.18) that she thought the diagram gave her

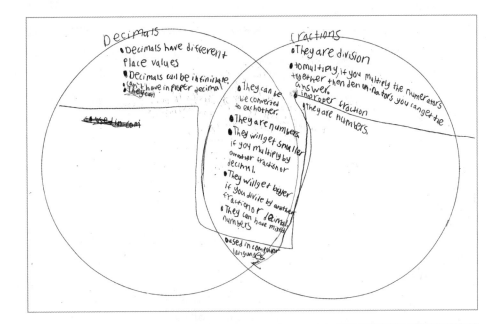

Figure 8.17
Kim's diagram

Figure 8.18
Kim's reflection on why she chose the diagram

Which tool did you use, venn diagram or same/difference chart, to organize your thinking? Why?

I used the venn diagram to organize my thinking. One way I did this was because the same different chart was way too small and you had to make it into little sections for decimals and fractions. But the venn diagram was much bigger and already had sections for fractions and decimals. Also you can clearly see what fractions and decimals have seperatly and what they have together because the same stuff is where the circles go together and different stuff is when the circles are apart. In conclusion venn diagrams are easier to use.

more space. She also noted that you could clearly identify what was true about both of them and what was true about one of them but not the other.

Nearly all the students wrote that they found decimals easier than fractions. Most of their reasons had to do with how similar working with decimals was to working with whole numbers. Finley (Figure 8.19) was one of two students who suggested that it depended on which operation you were using, because multiplication and division were easier with fractions.

Figure 8.19
Finley's reflection on whether fractions or decimals are easier

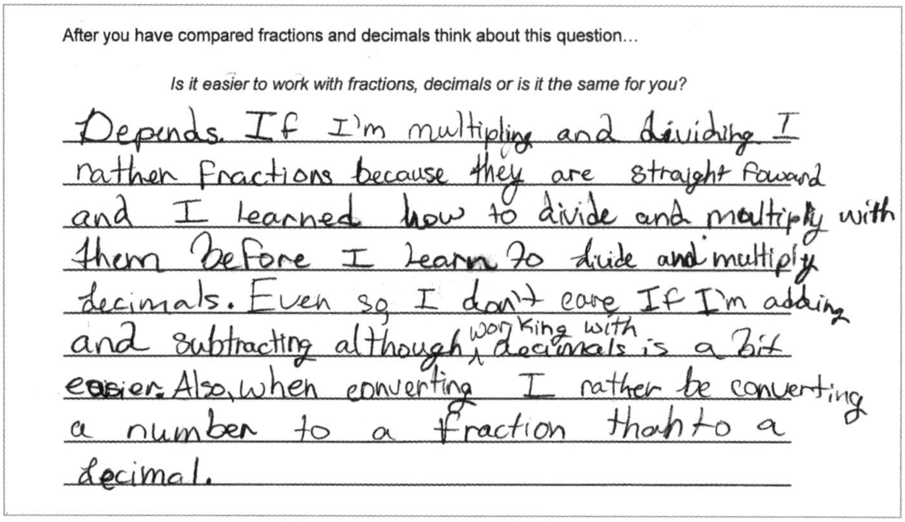

After you have compared fractions and decimals think about this question...

Is it easier to work with fractions, decimals or is it the same for you?

Depends. If I'm multipling and dividing I rathen fractions because they are straight foward and I learned how to divide and maltiply with them before I learn to dride and multiply decimals. Even so I don't care If I'm adding and subtracting although working with decimals is a bit easier. Also, when converting I rather be converting a number to a fraction than to a decimal.

Kathy's Reflection

This experience was much more intense than I expected. I don't usually have students make these types of comparisons, but it proved to be really worthwhile. Students were engaged and questioned their own ideas as well as the thinking of others. I hadn't expected that making the charts and diagrams would also involve reflective thinking, but it did. Students were stepping back and thinking more deeply about the similarities and differences between these two ways to record parts of wholes. It was as if they were suddenly looking through a wide-angle lens, and as they did so, they recognized more about what they knew.

I was surprised that students wrote almost exclusively about calculation techniques when they reflected on whether fractions or decimals were easier for them. I used the phrase to work with in my question. I wonder if their responses would have been different if I had written, Is it easier to use . . . Tomorrow I want to talk with them about using fractions and decimals in different contexts.

I wonder if they can identify situations in which we nearly always use fractions and those in which we nearly always use decimals.

Growth Over Time

As the year drew to a close, Maureen O'Connell was interested in having students reflect on how they thought and felt about math at the beginning of the year and how they thought and felt about it now. She asked a variety of students she worked with and encouraged teachers in her school to do the same. She often incorporated the phrases *I used to think* and *Now I think* suggested in *Making Thinking Visible* (Ritchhart, Church, and Morrison 2011).

I had the privilege of observing Maureen and first-grade teacher Andrea Welch help students reflect on their growth. Maureen had prepared a template for students to complete, and Andrea gave her students a recent sample of their work as well as one from the beginning of the year. It was amazing to see how different the older and newer examples looked. Yet I will always remember Samantha, who looked at her work and said, "I'm not sure. I mean, this is mine [holding up one piece of work], and this is mine [holding up the other sample.]" It was as though the only connection she made to the collective work was that she had indeed completed each one. Did she not see any other similarity or difference?

As we sat together, I asked Samantha to describe what she saw. In time, she was able to note many differences. This was a great reminder to me that we need to model for students how to look at their own work so that they can appreciate and recognize their growth. Samantha's earlier and more recent recordings are shown in Figure 8.20. The first is a solution to a number story about birds in

Figure 8.20
Samantha's early and later samples of work

I used a number grid.

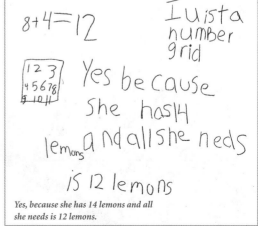

Yes, because she has 14 lemons and all she needs is 12 lemons.

trees: three in the first tree, two in the second, and one in the third. Samantha has recorded the one and the two. Her paper shows a 9. Perhaps she was trying to indicate the total of six birds and was confused about how to record the numeral, or perhaps she added the three trees to the six birds. Samantha giggled when she looked at the 9. She said, "I don't know what 9 is for. I make more sense now." Her later recording is in response to a number story that asks if fourteen lemons are enough if four are needed for one recipe and eight for another.

Figure 8.21
Uma's feelings about math

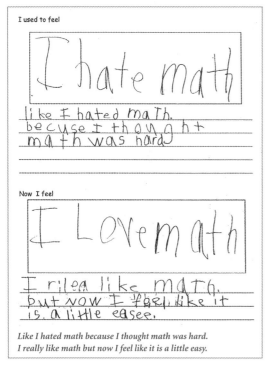

Like I hated math because I thought math was hard.
I really like math but now I feel like it is a little easy.

Figure 8.22
Maureen's _yet_ poster

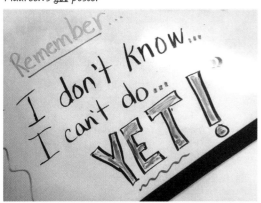

Samantha, as well as several other students, noted, *I used to draw pictures. But now I write words and number models.* Offering students an opportunity to review work over a range of time is a wonderful way for them to have tangible evidence of a year's worth of growth. Andrea told me that she, too, enjoyed taking the time to notice and acknowledge the wonderful strides her students had made since the beginning of the school year.

Students in this class also wrote about how they felt about math. I found it heartwarming that nearly all of them wrote that they used to feel that math was hard, but now they thought it was easy or easier. Uma's response is shown in Figure 8.21.

Carol Dweck (mentioned in Chapter 2) believes in the power of "yet" (TEDx Talk, September 12, 2014). She encourages us to open fixed-mindset thinking by changing a comment such as "I can't do this" to "I can't do this *yet*." Maureen O'Connell models this language herself, and expects her students to understand its importance and use it as well. In the beginning of the year, she wrote a message that highlighted *yet* on the whiteboard near where she works with small groups (Figure 8.22). She left it up throughout the year, and in the spring, during indoor recess, a small group of students created their own poster for her with a blue sticky note in the corner that says *to Mrs. O'Connell* (Figure 8.23).

Figure 8.23
Student-
made poster
for <u>yet</u>

It's clear that Maureen believes each of her students is capable of being successful. This is true for students of all ages with whom she works as a math specialist, but knowing that the fifth graders in her town are headed for middle school, she has been particularly adamant about maintaining this outlook with them. Collin's reflection (Figure 8.24) on how his thinking and feelings have changed indicates how much this phrase influenced him.

Figure 8.24
Collin's
reflection

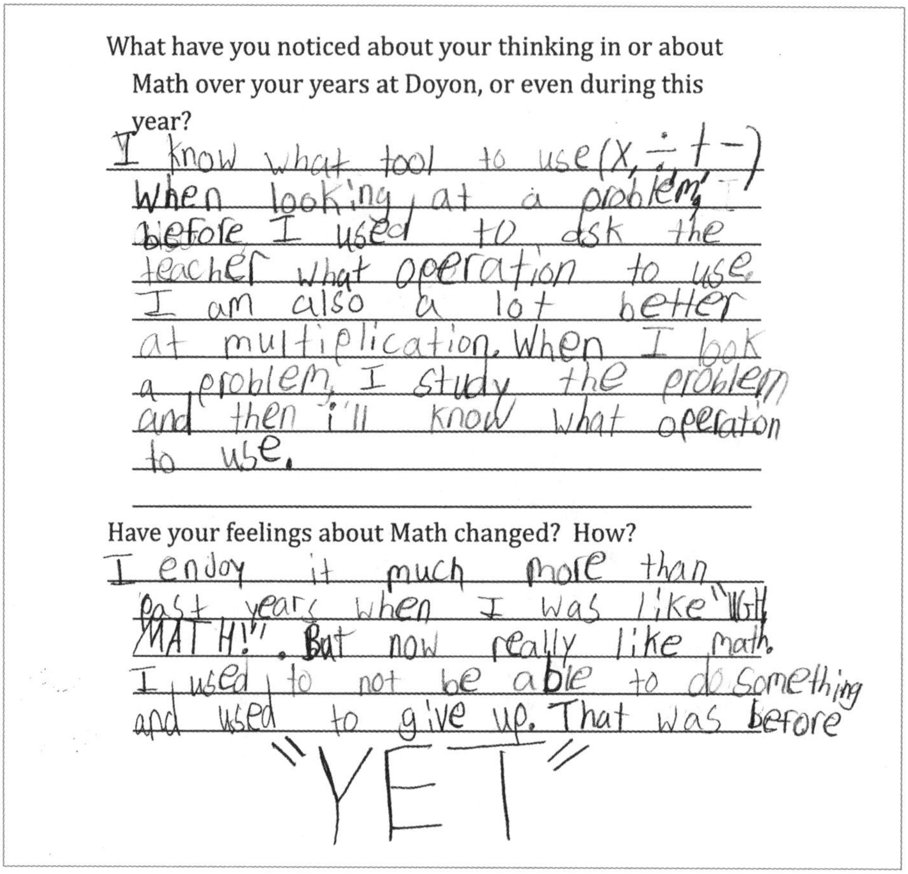

What have you noticed about your thinking in or about
Math over your years at Doyon, or even during this
year?

I know what tool to use (x, ÷, + -)
when looking at a problem.
before I used to ask the
teacher what operation to use.
I am also a lot better
at multiplication. When I look
a problem, I study the problem
and then i'll know what operaton
to use.

Have your feelings about Math changed? How?

I enjoy it much more than
past years when I was like "Ugh
MATH!". But now really like math.
I used to not be able to do something
and used to give up. That was before
"YET"

Reflecting on Why Students Should Write in Math Class

You may have already witnessed the power of students writing about math and think it is as essential as learning facts and checking for accuracy—or you may not have done this *yet*. For me, working with teachers and students to increase the frequency and variety of writing that students were doing in math class has been a tremendous privilege. Throughout this journey, I have become even more convinced of the power of writing to learn math. I am once again awed by and grateful for educators who are always discovering and willing to experiment with new ways to support their students, as well as the scope and significance of the mathematical ideas K–5 students cover and uncover on their path to mathematical understanding and competence. I am convinced, more than ever, that by including writing in math class with the same spirit with which talking has been embraced, we offer students a new way to explore, explain, defend, integrate, and reflect on their math learning. To that end, here are some ideas I would like to leave you with as you pursue this work with your students:

- Don't confuse students writing to show what they know with writing to learn. The goals are very different. In many schools, the former is overemphasized, and the latter is not given enough attention.
- When teachers are excited about writing in mathematics and show students how it is beneficial, both in the moment and over time, their students get excited, too.
- There are many ways for students to write about mathematics. Do not limit them to only explaining and/or justifying their thinking.
- Writing about mathematics can happen within literacy learning, too.
- There is never enough time to do all that we want. Choose wisely and make sure writing to learn math is among the choices you make.
- Writing is a powerful learning tool. Embrace it! Enjoy it! Let it help your students thrive!

References

Baker, Linda. 2012. "Metacognitive Strategies." In *International Guide to Student* Achievement, ed. John Hattie and Eric M. Anderman. New York: Routledge.

Bay-Williams, Jennifer M., and Stefanie Livers. 2009. "Supporting Math Vocabulary Acquisition." *Teaching Children Mathematics* 16(4): 238–45.

Barlow, Angela T., and Michael R. McCrory. 2011. "3 Strategies for Promoting Math Disagreements." *Teaching Children Mathematics* 17(9): 530–39.

Benjamin, Amy. 2013. *Math in Plain English: Literacy Strategies for the Mathematics Classroom.* New York: Routledge.

Boaler, Jo. 2015. "Evidence." https://www.youcubed.org/think-it-up/mistakes-grow-brain/.

Bruun, Faye, Joan Diaz, and Valerie Dykes. 2015. "The Language of Mathematics." *Teaching Children Mathematics* 21(9): 530–36.

Burns, Marilyn. 1995. *Writing in Math Class: A Resource Guide for Grade K–8.* Sausalito, CA: Math Solutions.

———. 1994. *The Greedy Triangle.* New York: Scholastic.

Calkins, Lucy, and Amanda Hartman. 2013. *Launching the Writing Workshop, Grade K Unit 1.* Portsmouth, NH: Heinemann.

Calkins, Lucy, and Kathleen Toban. 2015. "Research Clubs: Elephants, Penguins, and Frogs, Oh My!" In *Units of Study for Teaching Reading, Grade 3*. Portsmouth, NH: Heinemann.

Carpenter, Thomas P., Megan Loef Franke, and Linda Levi. 2003. *Thinking Mathematically: Integrating Arithmetic and Algebra in Elementary School*. Portsmouth, NH: Heinemann.

Casa, Tutita M., Janine M. Firmender, June Cahill, Fabiana Cardetti, Jeffrey M. Choppin, Jeremy Cohen, Shelbi Cole, et al. 2016. *Types of and Purposes for Elementary Mathematical Writing: Task Force Recommendations*. Retrieved from https://mathwriting.education.uconn.edu/home/elementary-task-force-recommendations/.

Center for Applied Special Technology. 2011. *Universal Design for Learning Guidelines version 2.0*. Wakefield, MA: CAST.

Chapin, Suzanne, Catherine O'Connor, and Nancy Anderson. 2003. *Classroom Discussions: Using Math Talk to Help Students Learn, Grades 1–6*. Sausalito, CA: Math Solutions.

Costa, Arthur L., and Bena Kallick, eds. 2008. *Learning and Leading with Habits of Mind: 16 Essential Characteristics for Success*. Association for Supervision and Curriculum.

Countryman, Joan. 1992. *Writing to Learn Mathematics: Strategies That Work, K–12*. Portsmouth, NH: Heinemann.

Dacey, Linda. 2012. *50 Leveled Math Problems, Level 4*. Huntington Beach, CA: Shell Education.

Dacey, Linda, and Lisa Donovan. 2013. *Strategies to Integrate the Arts in Mathematics*. Huntington Beach, CA: Shell Education.

Danielson, Christopher. 2016. *Which One Doesn't Belong? A Shapes Book*. Portland, ME: Stenhouse.

Daywalt, Drew. 2013. *The Day the Crayons Quit*. New York: Philomel Books.

Dodds, Dayle Ann. 1996. *The Shape of Things*. New York: Scholastic.

Dweck, Carol S. 2014. "The Power of Yet." TEDxNorrkölpin given on September 12. https://www.youtube.com/watch?v=J-swZaKN2Ic&list=PLAzptIch_kS4g1fdDRXCPF3QrF71g7dcv&index=12.

———. 2006. *Mindset: The New Psychology of Success*. New York: Ballantine Books.

Edwards, Sharon A., Robert W. Maloy, and Gordon Anderson. 2010. "Classroom Characters Coach Students to Success." *Teaching Children Mathematics* 16(6): 342–49.

Flynn, Mike. 2017. *Beyond Answers: Exploring Mathematical Practices with Young Children*. Portland, ME: Stenhouse.

Goldstone, Bruce. 2016. *Greater Estimations: A Fun Introduction to Estimating Large Numbers.* New York: Henry Holt.

Greenes, Carole E., Linda Schulman, and Rika Spungin. 1993. "Developing Sense about Numbers." *Arithmetic Teacher* 40(5): 279–84.

Hattie, John. 2008. *Visible Learning: A Synthesis of Over 800 Meta-analyses Relating to Achievement.* New York: Routledge.

Hosford, Kate. 2012. *Infinity and Me.* Minneapolis, MN: Carolrhoda Picture Books.

Jenkins, Steve. 2016. *Animals by the Numbers: A Book of Infographics.* Boston: HMH Books for Young Readers.

Kazemi, Elham, and Allison Hintz. 2014. *Intentional Talk: How to Structure and Lead Productive Mathematical Discussions.* Portland, ME: Stenhouse.

Kilpatrick, Jeremy, Jane Swafford, and Bradford Findell, eds. 2001. *Adding It Up: Helping Children Learn Mathematics.* Washington, DC: National Academy Press.

Kostos, Kathleen, and Eui-kyung Shin. 2010. "Using Math Journals to Enhance Second Graders' Communication of Mathematical Thinking." *Early Childhood Education Journal* 38(3): 223–31.

Marzano, Robert, Debra Pickering, and Jane E. Pollock. 2001. *Classroom Instruction That Works: Research-Based Strategies for Increasing Student Achievement.* Alexandria, VA: Association for Supervision and Curriculum Development.

Marzano, Robert. 2007. *The Art and Science of Teaching.* Alexandria, VA: Association for Supervision and Curriculum Development.

Menotti, Andreas. 2012. *How Many Jelly Beans?* San Francisco, CA: Chronicle Books.

Michelson, Richard. 2000. *Ten Times Better.* New York: Marshall Cavendish Children's Books.

Moschkovich, Judit. 2012. "Mathematics, the Common Core, and Language: Recommendations for Mathematics Instruction for ELs Aligned with the Common Core." Retrieved from http://ell.stanford.edu/sites/default/files/pdf/academic-papers/02-JMoschkovich%20Math%20FINAL_bound%20with%20appendix.pdf.

Murray, Donald M. 1969. "The Explorers of Inner Space." *The English Journal* 58(6): 908–11.

National Governors Association Center for Best Practices, Council of Chief State School Officers. 2010a. Common Core State Standards for Mathematics. Washington, DC: NGO/CCSSO. http://www.corestandards.org/wp-content/uploads /Math_Standards.pdf.

————. 2010b. Common Core State Standards for English, Language Arts & Literacy in History/Social Studies, Science and Technical Subjects (CCS-SELA). Washington, DC: NGO/CCSSO.

Pappas, Theoni. 1993. *Math Talk: Mathematical Ideas in Poems for Two Voices.* San Carlos, CA: Wide World.

Parrish, Sherry. 2014. *Number Talks: Whole Number Computation, Grades K–5.* Sausalito, CA: Math Solutions.

Pugalee, David K. 2005. *Writing to Develop Mathematical Understanding.* Norwood, MA: Christopher-Gordon.

Ray, Katie Wood, and Matt Glover. 2008. *Already Ready: Nurturing Writers in Preschool and Kindergarten.* Portsmouth, NH: Heinemann.

Reid, Margarette S. 1990. *The Button Box.* New York: Dutton Children's Books.

Ritchhart, Ron, Mark Church, and Karin Morrison. 2011. *Making Thinking Visible: How to Promote Engagement, Understanding, and Independence for All Learners.* San Francisco: Jossey-Bass.

Russell, Susan Jo, Deborah Schifter, Virginia Bastable, Traci Higgins, and Reva Kasman. 2017. *But Why Does It Work? Mathematical Argument in the Elementary Classroom.* Portsmouth, NH: Heinemann.

Smith, Margaret S., and Mary Kay Stein. 2011. *5 Practices for Orchestrating Productive Mathematical Discussions.* Reston, VA: National Council of Teachers of Mathematics.

TERC. 2008. *Investigations in Number, Data, and Space.* 2nd ed. Glenville, IL: Pearson Scott.

Tompert, Ann. 1990. *Grandfather Tang's Story: A Tale Told with Tangrams.* New York: Dragonfly Books.

Wiggins, Grant. 2012. "Seven Keys to Effective Feedback. *Educational Leadership* 70(1): 10–16.

Zager, Tracy Johnston. 2017. *Becoming the Math Teacher You Wish You'd Had: Ideas and Strategies from Vibrant Classrooms.* Portland, ME: Stenhouse.

Index